CliffsN

The Fountainhead

By Andrew Bernstein, Ph.D.

IN THIS BOOK

- Learn about the Life and Background of the Author
- Preview an Introduction to the Novel
- Explore themes, character development, and recurring images in the Critical Commentaries
- Examine in-depth Character Analyses
- Acquire an understanding of the novel with Critical Essays
- Reinforce what you learn with CliffsNotes Review
- Find additional information to further your study in the CliffsNotes Resource Center and online at www.cliffsnotes.com

Hungry Minds™

Best-Selling Books • Digital Downloads • e-Books • Answer Networks • e-Newsletters • Branded Web Sites • e-Learning

New York, NY • Cleveland, OH • Indianapolis, IN

About the Author

Andrew Bernstein holds a Ph.D. in Philosophy from the Graduate School of the City University of New York. He teaches Philosophy at Pace University in Pleasantville, New York, and at the State University of New York at Purchase. Dr. Bernstein is a speaker for the Ayn Rand Institute and lectures on Ayn Rand's novels throughout the United States.

Publisher's Acknowledgments

Editorial

Project Editor: Elizabeth Netedu Kuball

Acquisitions Editor: Gregory W. Tubach

Glossary Editors: The editors and staff of Webster's New World Dictionaries

Editorial Administrator: Michelle Haker

Production

Indexer: York Production Services, Inc.

Proofreader: York Production Services, Inc.

Hungry Minds Indianapolis Production

CliffsNotes™ *The Fountainhead*

Published by:

Hungry Minds, Inc.
909 Third Avenue
New York, NY 10022

www.hungryminds.com

www.cliffsnotes.com (CliffsNotes Web site)

ISBN: 0-7645-8558-4

Printed in the United States of America

10 9 8 7 6 5 4 3

1V/QS/RQ/QR/IN

Distributed in the United States by Hungry Minds, Inc.

Distributed by CDG Books Canada Inc. for Canada; by Transworld Publishers Limited in the United Kingdom; by IDG Norge Books for Norway; by IDG Sweden Books for Sweden; by IDG Books Australia Publishing Corporation Pty. Ltd. for Australia and New Zealand; by TransQuest Publishers Pte Ltd. for Singapore, Malaysia, Thailand, Indonesia, and Hong Kong; by Gotop Information Inc. for Taiwan; by ICG Muse, Inc. for Japan; by Norma Comunicaciones S.A. for Columbia; by Intersoft for South Africa; by Eyrolles for France; by International Thomson Publishing for Germany, Austria and Switzerland; by Distribuidora Cuspide for Argentina; by LR International for Brazil; by Galileo Libros for Chile; by Ediciones ZETA S.C.R. Ltda. for Peru; by WS Computer Publishing Corporation, Inc., for the Philippines; by Contemporanea de Ediciones for Venezuela; by Express Computer Distributors for the Caribbean and West Indies; by Micronesia Media Distributor, Inc. for Micronesia; by Grupo Editorial Norma S.A. for Guatemala; by Chips Computadoras S.A. de C.V. for Mexico; by Editorial Norma de Panama S.A. for Panama; by American Bookshops for Finland. Authorized Sales Agent: Anthony Rudkin Associates for the Middle East and North Africa.

Library of Congress Cataloging-in-Publication Data

Bernstein, Andrew.

CliffsNotes, The Fountainhead / by Andrew Bernstein.

p. cm.

Includes bibliographical references and index.

ISBN 0-7645-8558-7 (alk. paper)

1. Rand, Ayn. Fountainhead--Examinations--Study guides. 2. Didactic fiction, American--Examinations--Study guides. I. Title: Fountainhead. II. Title.

PS3535.A547 F6933 2000
813'.52--dc21   00–035026
                                                           CIP

For general information on Hungry Minds' products and services please contact our Customer Care department; within the U.S. at 800-762-2974, outside the U.S. at 317-572-3993 or fax 317-572-4002.

For sales inquiries and resellers information, including discounts, premium and bulk quantity sales and foreign language translations please contact our Customer Care department at 800-434-3422, fax 317-572-4002 or write to Hungry Minds, Inc., Attn: Customer Care department, 10475 Crosspoint Boulevard, Indianapolis, IN 46256.

For information on licensing foreign or domestic rights, please contact our Sub-Rights Customer Care department at 212-884-5000.

For information on using Hungry Minds' products and services in the classroom or for ordering examination copies, please contact our Educational Sales department at 800-434-2086 or fax 317-572-4005.

Please contact our Public Relations department at 212-884-5163 for press review copies or 212-884-5000 for author interviews and other publicity information or fax 212-884-5400.

For authorization to photocopy items for corporate, personal, or educational use, please contact Copyright Clearance Center, 222 Rosewood Drive, Danvers, MA 01923, or fax 978-750-4470.

Table of Contents

How to Use This Book

CliffsNotes *The Fountainhead* supplements the original work, giving you background information about the author, an introduction to the novel, a graphical character map, critical commentaries, expanded glossaries, and a comprehensive index. CliffsNotes Review tests your comprehension of the original text and reinforces learning with questions and answers, practice projects, and more. For further information on Ayn Rand and *The Fountainhead*, check out the CliffsNotes Resource Center.

CliffsNotes provides the following icons to highlight essential elements of particular interest:

Reveals the underlying themes in the work.

Helps you to more easily relate to or discover the depth of a character.

Uncovers elements such as setting, atmosphere, mystery, passion, violence, irony, symbolism, tragedy, foreshadowing, and satire.

Enables you to appreciate the nuances of words and phrases.

Don't Miss Our Web Site

Discover classic literature as well as modern-day treasures by visiting the CliffsNotes Web site at www.cliffsnotes.com. You can obtain a quick download of a CliffsNotes title, purchase a title in print form, browse our catalog, or view online samples.

You'll also find interactive tools that are fun and informative, links to interesting Web sites, tips, articles, and additional resources to help you, not only for literature, but for test prep, finance, careers, computers, and Internet too. See you at www.cliffsnotes.com!

LIFE AND BACKGROUND OF THE AUTHOR

Personal Background

Ayn Rand was born Alisa Rosenbaum in 1905 in St. Petersburg, Russia. Rand was raised in an upper-middle-class, European-oriented family, in the midst of the mysticism and nationalism of Holy Mother Russia (the fervent faith in Christianity, in the sinfulness of man, and in the moral mission of Russia to convert the world to its religious philosophy). Having taught herself to read, Rand, at the age of nine, became captivated by the heroism in a French-language serial adventure entitled *The Mysterious Valley*. At the age of eleven, Rand decided to become a writer, inspired especially by Victor Hugo's novels. Hugo's writing helped arm her against the fatalistic view of life that dominated Russia, a country she later described as "an accidental cesspool of civilization."

Education and Early Life

In February of 1917, Ayn Rand witnessed the first shots of the Russian Revolution, and later that year witnessed the Bolshevik Revolution as well. In order to escape the fighting, her family went to the Crimea, where Rand finished high school. The final Communist victory brought the confiscation of her father's pharmacy and periods of near-starvation. When introduced to American history in her last year of high school, Rand immediately took America as her model of what a nation of free men could be. Her love for the West—especially America—was fueled by the Viennese operettas and American and German films, which the Soviets temporarily allowed to be shown.

When Rand and her family returned from the Crimea, she entered the University of Petrograd to study philosophy and history, graduating in 1924. She entered the State Institute for Cinema Arts in 1924 to study screenwriting, as a step to becoming a novelist. During this period, Rand produced her first formal writings, essays about Hollywood, published in 1999 by The Ayn Rand Institute Press as *Russian Writings on Hollywood*.

Immigration to the United States

In late 1925, Ayn Rand obtained permission to leave the Soviet Union for a visit to relatives in the United States, on the pretext of learning the American film business. After six months with relatives in

Chicago, she moved to Hollywood to pursue a career as a screenwriter. On her second day there, she had a chance meeting with her favorite American director, Cecil B. DeMille, who took her to the set of his epic film, *The King of Kings*, and gave her a job, first as an extra, then as a script reader. During the next week at the studio, she met an actor, Frank O'Connor, whom she married in 1929; they were married until his death fifty years later.

Career Highlights

After struggling for several years at various non-writing jobs, including one in the wardrobe department at the RKO film studio, Rand sold her first screenplay, *Red Pawn*, to Universal Studios in 1932. In the same year, Rand saw her first stage play, *Night of January 16th*, produced in Hollywood and then on Broadway. Her first novel, *We the Living*, was completed in 1933. The most autobiographical of Rand's novels, *We the Living* was rejected as too anti-Communist and wasn't published in the United States until 1936. In 1937, Rand devoted a few weeks to write her novella, *Anthem*, which was soon published in England but was not published in the United States until 1947, ten years later.

Although positively reviewed, neither *We the Living* nor *Anthem* garnered high sales. Not until the publication of *The Fountainhead* did Ayn Rand achieve fame. Rand began writing *The Fountainhead* in 1935, taking seven years to complete the book. In the hero of *The Fountainhead*, architect Howard Roark, she presented for the first time the kind of hero whose depiction was the chief goal of her writing: the ideal man, man "as he could be and ought to be." *The Fountainhead* was rejected by twelve publishers but finally accepted by Bobbs-Merrill. Although published in 1943, *The Fountainhead* made history by becoming a bestseller two years later, through word-of-mouth, and it gained for its author lasting recognition as a champion of individualism.

Ayn Rand returned to Hollywood in late 1943 to write the screenplay for *The Fountainhead*, but war-time restrictions delayed production until 1948. Working part-time as a screenwriter for producer Hal Wallis, Rand wrote such scripts as *Love Letters* and *You Came Along*, and she began her major novel, *Atlas Shrugged*, in 1946. In 1951, Rand moved permanently back to New York City and devoted herself full-time to the completion of the novel *Atlas Shrugged*. Despite extremely negative reviews, *Atlas Shrugged* quickly became a best-seller.

Rand's Philosophy: Objectivism

After the publication of *Atlas Shrugged* in 1957, Ayn Rand realized that she would have to identify the philosophy that made her heroes possible. She termed this philosophy Objectivism and described it as "a philosophy for living on earth." Rand offered private courses on both fiction and nonfiction writing and, in 1958, helped form an institute to teach her philosophy. For the remaining years of her life, Rand devoted herself to nonfiction writing, penning and editing a number of articles for her periodicals. These articles later appeared in numerous philosophic collections, including ethics (*The Virtue of Selfishness*), politics (*Capitalism: the Unknown Ideal*), aesthetics (*The Romantic Manifesto*), and the theory of knowledge (*Introduction to Objectivist Epistemology*). At the time of her death in 1982, Rand was working on a television miniseries *of Atlas Shrugged*.

A controversial novelist and philosopher—especially in academic circles—Ayn Rand attained widespread recognition, as indicated by a 1991 survey placing *Atlas Shrugged* as second only to the Bible as the most influential book among American readers. The Ayn Rand Society (a subgroup of the American Philosophical Association), an Ayn Rand first-class postage stamp (printed in 1999), and an Academy Award-nominated documentary about her life (*Ayn Rand: A Sense of Life*, 1997) also serve as proof of her influence.

INTRODUCTION TO THE NOVEL

Introduction

The Fountainhead serves as an excellent introduction to both Ayn Rand's writing and her philosophy of Objectivism. All of the major intellectual themes that inform Rand's fiction and her subsequent philosophy are presented clearly in this novel.

Having grown up in the totalitarian dictatorship of the Soviet Union, holding an impassioned belief in political freedom and the rights of the individual, Ayn Rand wrote *The Fountainhead* as a tribute to the creative freethinker. Its hero, Howard Roark, is an innovative architect, a man whose brilliant and radically new designs are not understood and are rejected by the majority of society. Roark, like many inventors and creative thinkers of history, struggles to win acceptance for his ideas against the tradition-bound masses, who follow established norms and are fearful of change. The theme, as Ayn Rand states it, is individualism versus collectivism, not in politics but in men's souls. The book is about the conflict between those who think for themselves and those who allow others to dominate their lives.

According to Ayn Rand, the goal of her writing is the presentation of an ideal man. Howard Roark is the first such figure in her novels. His independence, his commitment to his own rational thinking, and his integrity mark him as a distinctive Ayn Rand hero. Rand described herself as a "man-worshiper," as one who revered man at his highest and best. She held man's creative mind as sacred, and consequently admired the great original thinkers of mankind—the artists, scientists, and inventors, such as Michelangelo, Newton, and Edison. In Rand's fiction, she illustrates the heroic battles such great individuals have to go through, both to develop their new ideas and methods and to struggle against a conservative society that rejects them. Ayn Rand presents her heroes as ends in themselves, inviting her readers to simply witness and savor the sight of human greatness. "My purpose, first cause and prime mover is the portrayal of Howard Roark . . . *as an end in himself*—not as a means to any further end. Which, incidentally, is the greatest value I could ever offer a reader." Her portrayal of such a character is of great value, because the sight of a dauntless hero performing notable deeds is an uplifting experience, one that requires no further explanation or validation. She points out that, as a benign secondary consequence, a reader witnessing the life of Howard Roark may be inspired to seek his own heroic achievements.

Roark, as a freethinking individual, is opposed by sundry collectivists—some who believe that a person should conform to others, some who believe that a person should rebel against others, and some who believe that, politically, we should have a Fascist or Communist dictatorship in which the individual is utterly subordinate to the will of the people. Regarding this aspect of the book, Rand sets her hero against various collectivist ideas that existed—and to some degree continue to exist—in the United States.

The obvious example of collectivism in *The Fountainhead* is the political one. Ellsworth Toohey, the novel's villain, is a Marxist intellectual, preaching socialism to the masses. He holds that an individual has no value in himself but exists solely to serve his brothers. As Ayn Rand wrote the novel, in the 1930s, collectivism was rapidly engulfing the world. First the Communists took over her native Russia, then the Fascists came to power in Italy, then Hitler and the National Socialists took political control of Germany. On September 1, 1939, Nazi Germany and the Soviet Union, as allies, invaded Poland, plunging mankind into the most destructive war of its history. In the early 1940s, collectivism appeared to be on the threshold of military conquest of large portions of the globe. In the United States, many intellectuals, politicians, labor leaders, and businessmen thought of the Communist and Nazi systems as "noble experiments," as new attempts to emphasize an individual's moral responsibilities to his fellow man. Before the war, there was ideological support in the United States for both the Communists and the Nazis; even after the war, support among the intellectuals continued for Communism and does to this day. Ayn Rand wrote *The Fountainhead*, at one level, as a fervent warning to her fellow man of the unmitigated horrors of collectivism, whether of the Nazi, Fascist, or Communist variety; the evils that result in concentration camps; the extermination of millions of innocent victims; and the precipitation of world war. Ayn Rand witnessed these horrors firsthand in Europe; she wrote *The Fountainhead*, in part, to prevent their recurrence in America.

But *The Fountainhead* is not fundamentally about politics. The book warns against a more subtle manifestation of collectivism, one that underlies the political danger and makes that danger possible. Although all human beings have minds, many people choose not to use theirs, looking instead to others for guidance. Many people prefer to be led in their personal lives by an authority figure—be it parents, teachers, clergymen, or others. Those who prefer to be led by authority figures are conformists, refusing the responsibility of thought and self-directed motivation, taking the path of least resistance in life. In the character of Peter Keating, a conventional architect who goes by public taste, Ayn

Rand provides an incisive glimpse into the soul of such an abject follower. The picture is frightening. Keating, in many ways an average American status seeker, desires acclaim from others. In exchange for social approval, he is willing to sacrifice any and all of his personal convictions. He becomes a blind follower of the power broker, Ellsworth Toohey, and in so doing reveals the mentality of the millions of "true believers" who blindly follow a Jim Jones, a Sun Myung Moon, or an Adolf Hitler. Ayn Rand shows that conformity, a widespread phenomenon in contemporary American society, is one of the underlying causes of collectivist dictatorship.

In *The Fountainhead*, Rand also shows that nonconformity, often thought to be the opposite of blind obedience, is merely a variation on the same theme. In a variety of minor characters (Lois Cook, Ike the Genius, Gus Webb), all devotees of Toohey, Rand demonstrates the essence of nonconformity: an unthinking rebellion against the values and convictions of others. The nonconformist, too, places the beliefs of others first, before his own thinking; he merely reacts *against* them, instead of following them. It is no accident that Ayn Rand shows these rebels as followers of Toohey, because nonconformists, placing others first, always cluster into private enclaves that inevitably demand rigid obedience to their own set of rules. Nonconformists value freethinking no more than does the herd of conformists. The nonconformist characters of the novel are fictional examples of historical movements of the early twentieth century. They are predominantly writers and artists who rebel against grammar, coherent sentences, and representational art in the same way that the surrealists, expressionists, and Dadaists did in actual fact. This band of real-life rebels, not surprisingly, centered in Weimar, Germany, in the 1920s. Outwardly, some opposed Hitler. But at a deeper level, their blind rebelliousness against others and their slavish conformity to their own little subgroup fostered a herd mentality similar to that of the conformists. The nonconformists, too, were part of the culture that spawned the Nazis. This is why, in *The Fountainhead*, when Toohey is chided for cultivating a circle of "rabid individualists," he merely laughs and responds: "Do you really think so?" He knows that a thinker like Roark is an individualist; posturing nonconformists like Lois Cook are mere rebels against the crowd.

The issue of conformity in the story relates to another real-life movement of the time. *The Fountainhead* takes place in America in the 1920s and 1930s. Roark and his mentor, Henry Cameron, are early designers of the modern style. Although the book is not historical fiction, and the lives of Cameron and Roark are not based on the lives of

When non-conformity is its own conformity — rebelling against the norm, just for the sake of rebellion real-life individuals, their struggles parallel the battles waged by Louis Sullivan and Frank Lloyd Wright. In the late-nineteenth and early-twentieth centuries, the architectural style that still dominated American building was Classical. American architects largely copied Greek and Roman designs (or those of other historical periods such as the Renaissance). Louis Sullivan (1856–1924) was one of the first to build in what became known as the modern style. Generally held to be the father of modern architecture and, in particular, of the skyscraper, Sullivan waged a long battle for his ideas against conventional standards. Ayn Rand scholar David Harriman, editor of *The Journals of Ayn Rand*, points out that Sullivan's life serves as a "concrete inspiration" for the character of Henry Cameron. Harriman also notes that Frank Lloyd Wright (1869–1959), the greatest of the modern designers, is famous for his "strikingly original designs." Wright was a fiercely independent individual, who refused to collaborate on his work and who learned early in his career not to compromise. Although the events of Roark's life are not identical to the events of Wright's, in the broad sense Wright does serve as the model for Howard Roark. Cameron and Roark, in the novel, struggle against characters like the Dean of Stanton Institute, who believes that all the great ideas in architecture have been discovered already by the designers of the past, and that contemporary architects are simply to copy those ideas. Sullivan and Wright, in real life, battled against similar instances of conformity. Though important similarities between Rand's fictional characters and Sullivan and Wright do exist, it is important to remember that Roark and Cameron are exemplars of innovativeness and independent thought; they are not fictionalized versions of Frank Lloyd Wright and Louis Sullivan.

In her previous novels, Ayn Rand had also glorified the heroism of the freethinking human mind, although in different forms. Her first novel, *We the Living*, published in 1936, tells the story of three individuals who dare to think for themselves in the Communist dictatorship of Soviet Russia. Its heroine, Kira Arguonova, is similar to the author; she is an independently thinking young woman, fiercely opposed to the totalitarian state in which she exists. But Kira desires to be an engineer in a society in which neither her bourgeois background nor her freethinking mind is welcome. Despite being an outstanding student, she is expelled from engineering school. The story focuses on her relationships with two men—Leo Kovalensky, the aristocrat whom she loves, and Andrei Taganov, the Communist who loves her. Leo is a brilliant young scholar, but his aristocratic family and individualistic views leave him no future in the Soviet Union. Andrei, an honest man who believes sincerely in the ideals of the Bolshevik Revolution, witnesses the harsh fate to which Kira is condemned, and must question the virtue of the Communist principles for which he has always stood. *We the Living* shows the fate of freethinking men and women in a totalitarian state.

Her second book, the novella, *Anthem,* published in 1938, also takes place in a collectivist dictatorship—but in an unspecified future. The dominance of the group over the individual is so absolute in this society that it has even outlawed the word "I." Individuals, referring to themselves in the first person, use the word "we." The story centers around one individual who refuses to obey the all-powerful state, but who, contrary to its wishes, becomes a scientist. With independent thought stifled, this society has lost all technological progress and reverted to a primitive condition. The hero reinvents the electric light, but is condemned to death for the crime of thinking for himself. Further, contrary to the state's decree, he dares to love a woman of his own choosing. In both love and work, he thinks independently, refusing to obey, unwilling to surrender the things most precious to him. Ayn Rand shows in *Anthem* that all the values that make human life valuable and joyous come from the individual, not from society.

In both *We the Living* and *Anthem*, the independent heroes are pitted against a collectivist dictatorship; in both books the theme is political, emphasizing the necessity of freedom for human progress and happiness. But the theme in *The Fountainhead* is deeper and more complex. It is psychological and epistemological. It concerns the way in which individuals choose to use their minds—whether they think and value independently or whether they allow their lives to be dominated, in one form or another, by the beliefs of others. The story of innovative architect Howard Roark, and his lifelong battle against a society committed to traditional forms of design, *The Fountainhead* glorifies the great original thinkers of history. Ayn Rand's subsequent *Atlas Shrugged*, published in 1957, carries further the same idea. It shows what happens when the thinkers go on strike—when the Howard Roark types, the inventors, scientists, and men of independent judgment—refuse to practice their professions in a world that expects them to comply. Ayn Rand's masterpiece, *Atlas Shrugged* shows the role of the mind in man's existence—not merely in the life of one rational individual, as in *The Fountainhead*, but in the life of an entire culture. All of her books defend man's mind, and uphold the need for an uncompromising independence of thought.

The history of *The Fountainhead* is like an example of its own theme. It was rejected by twelve publishers. Some thought that it was too intellectual, that there was no market for such a book among a reading public that was interested only in stories of physical action. Others rejected it because it glorified individualism and repudiated the collectivist ideals so popular among modern intellectuals. But Ayn Rand refused to alter her story or dilute her theme. Finally, the book was read by Archibald Ogden, an editor at Bobbs-Merrill. Like an independent-minded Ayn Rand hero, Ogden loved the book and fought for it against dissenting thought in the company. Despite the opposition, Ogden staked his career on this book. It was published in 1943 and made history several years later by becoming a best-seller through word of mouth. It was made into a successful film in 1949 with Gary Cooper as Howard Roark and Patricia Neal as Dominique Francon. By the end of the twentieth century, the book that was "too intellectual" had sold over six million copies and touched the lives of countless readers. To this day, it sells well over a hundred thousand copies every year. The Ayn Rand Institute's high school essay contest on *The Fountainhead,* initiated in 1986, averages three thousand essays per year. A poll conducted jointly in 1991 by the Library of Congress and the Book-of-the-Month Club showed that *Atlas Shrugged* was the second most influential book in the lives of the respondents (behind only the Bible) and showed *The Fountainhead* among the top twenty.

Today, *The Fountainhead* has achieved the status of a modern classic. It is taught in college literature and philosophy courses, as well as in high school English classes. *The Fountainhead* continues to be an example of its own theme: the struggle for acceptance of great new ideas in human society. But, in principle and in the long run, truth wins out. Despite continuing intellectual opposition to Ayn Rand's ideas, *The Fountainhead* has gained recognition as one of the great novels of American literature. Its theme of glorifying the independent mind not only captures the essence of the American spirit but, more fundamentally, expresses the deep human yearning for freedom. *The Fountainhead* is a theme and a novel that will live forever.

A Brief Synopsis

The Fountainhead takes place in the United States, mostly in New York City, during the 1920s and 1930s. It chronicles the struggles of the innovative architect Howard Roark in his effort to achieve success on his own terms.

As the story opens, twenty-one-year-old Roark is expelled from the Stanton Institute of Technology for "insubordination." Most faculty and administration members want him to design in traditional styles, but Roark has his own ideas. On the other hand, Peter Keating, a classmate of Roark's and the son of the woman whose boardinghouse Roark lives in, though lacking Roark's brilliance and love of architecture, gives the professors exactly what they want and graduates as valedictorian with high honors.

After leaving Stanton, Roark goes to work for Henry Cameron, an elderly and cantankerous genius, whose ideas are far ahead of their time. Cameron is a commercial failure, but an uncompromising man of integrity. Though a successful architect in the 1880s, Cameron's ideas became increasingly revolutionary, resulting finally in the birth of the skyscraper. He is one of the first to design buildings that tower over others, and the first to insist that a tall building should look tall. Where other architects use every device they can to make their tall buildings appear shorter, Cameron openly flaunts his skyscrapers' height. When American society falls under the sway of the Classical styles highlighted in the Columbian Exposition of 1892, Cameron's modernist ideas are rejected. Compounding the problem is Cameron's contemptuous rejection of those not open to change. His hostility only increases the difficulty that a public fearful of progress has in recognizing his genius. Roark works for him for three years (until Cameron's health fails) and learns to perfect the great and original talent he possesses.

After graduating from Stanton, Keating works for Guy Francon, the most successful and prestigious architect in the country. Francon is a mediocre architect who copies from the designers of the past; but he gives the public what it's used to, and, with a superb mastery of the social graces, he wines and dines prospective clients at New York's most exclusive restaurants. Francon is a phony, who teaches Keating only about manipulating and influencing people, not about building honestly and effectively.

Francon has a beautiful young daughter, Dominique, who possesses a mind of her own. Brilliant and outspoken, she is brutally frank in criticizing the buildings of her father and his young protégé. Dominique writes a column devoted to design and interior decorating in *The New York Banner*, a daily newspaper owned by the powerful publisher, Gail Wynand. Dominique is a passionate idealist who recognizes and reveres the human potential for greatness. But finding little of it in the world—indeed, finding everywhere the triumph of vulgar mediocrity—she becomes disillusioned. Dominique believes that true nobility has no chance to succeed in a world dominated by the mindless and the corrupt. She recognizes and loathes the unscrupulous pandering engaged in by Keating and her father—and states her convictions openly. But Keating, smitten with the way in which her beauty and elegance impress other people, proposes marriage. Dominique replies that if she ever seeks to punish herself for some terrible crime she's committed, she will accept his offer.

Despite Dominique's recognition of his fraudulent methods, Keating enjoys great early success. By the manipulation of fellow employees, Keating rises in Francon's firm until, after only several years, he is the company's chief designer. Though not adept at design, Keating knows someone who is: Howard Roark, whose love of buildings is so great that he cannot refuse any opportunity to improve one. Roark helps Keating in his design work. But now, Keating has his sights set on becoming Francon's partner, a position currently held by the sickly Lucius Heyer. At this time comes the announcement for the Cosmo-Slotnick Building, a competition held by a Hollywood company to design the "world's most beautiful building." Francon trusts Keating to win; Keating knows he cannot do it, so he turns to Roark for help. Roark designs a brilliant and simple plan for his building, to which Keating adds his customary ostentatious ornamentation. Keating believes his eclectic hodgepodge of conflicting styles has no chance to win; he must get the partnership now, while Francon still trusts him. He berates Heyer, screaming at the old man to retire, causing the stroke the doctors had feared. Heyer dies, having left the charming Keating his money. Keating wins the Cosmo-Slotnick competition. Francon makes him partner. Keating is now wealthy, famous, and a partner in the country's most prestigious architectural firm.

Roark, meanwhile, struggles to find employment after Cameron's retirement. His brief tenure at Francon's firm ends when he refuses to design as Francon wishes him to. For a long period of time, Roark cannot find employment with any architect. Eventually, he is hired by John Erik Snyte, an eclectic builder who is not wedded to any specific school of design. Snyte is content to give the public whatever it desires. He employs specialists in various schools of design—Classical, Gothic, Renaissance—and wants Roark to be his modernist. Snyte allows his designers freedom to design in their specialties, but then combines their ideas into one finished product of clashing principles. Roark can design as he likes at Snyte's, but he will never see a building erected as he creates it. Eventually, the newspaperman, Austen Heller, recognizes his talent and hires him to build a private home. Roark opens his own office, but his designs are too revolutionary, and he receives very few commissions. When Roark turns down the commission for the important Manhattan Bank Building rather than permit the adulteration of his design, he is destitute. He closes his office temporarily and goes to work in a granite quarry in Connecticut.

The quarry is owned by Guy Francon. That summer, Dominique vacations at the family estate bordering the property. Upon meeting Roark, Dominique notices immediately the taut lines of his body and the scornful look of his eyes. Though at a conscious level, Dominique believes he may be an ex-convict like others of the work gang, at some deeper level she knows better. The way he holds himself and moves, his posture and mannerisms, his countenance and the look in his eyes all convey a proud dignity that would not stoop to the commission of crimes. She is deeply drawn to him and initiates a pursuit that results in their passionate lovemaking. But despite her profound attraction and aggressive pursuit, she is afraid of a love relationship with him. She ardently desires their sexual relationship, but almost as intensely fears it. She both physically resists Roark when he finally comes to her and experiences their lovemaking—"the thing she had thought about, had expected"—as the most powerful experience of her life. Dominique's inner conflict torments her, and, despite the love between them, it is years before they can happily be together. Before their relationship fully gets under way at the quarry, Roark's whereabouts are discovered by Roger Enright, an innovative businessman who wants Roark to design a new type of apartment building. Roark leaves the quarry and returns to New York. Even then, he finds himself thinking of Dominique.

The construction of the Enright House brings Roark recognition and further commissions. Anthony Cord, a successful Wall Street businessman, hires him to build his first office building, a fifty-story skyscraper in the center of Manhattan. Kent Lansing, a member of the board formed to build a luxury hotel on Central Park South, wants Roark and fights for him. Eventually, he wins, and Roark signs a contract to build the Aquitania Hotel. Although construction of the Aquitania is eventually stopped due to legal wrangles, Kent Lansing vows to win control of the project and complete it. Roark's growing fame attracts the attention of architectural critic Ellsworth Toohey, who is threatened by his unbending independence of spirit. Toohey, who seeks power over the architectural profession, attempts to end the career of this individualist who will not obey. He influences a wealthy lackey, Hopton Stoddard, to hire Roark to build a temple. Knowing that Roark's design will be breathtakingly original, Toohey plots to attack it as contrary to all established religious principles, thereby turning Roark into an enemy of religion. Because Roark is an atheist, Toohey coaches Stoddard regarding the best means to approach Roark to build a religious structure. He has Stoddard say, "But you're a profoundly religious man, Mr. Roark—in your own way. I can see that in your buildings." Roark accepts the commission to build a temple to the heroic human spirit.

At this point, Roark's career is on an upswing. He designs a masterpiece for the Stoddard Temple, as Toohey knew he would. He hires Steven Mallory to do the sculpture for the Temple. Mallory is a brilliant young talent, who sculpts in the Classic Greek style, emphasizing the nobility and grandeur of man. Dominique poses nude for the Temple's central piece of sculpture, and Mallory captures both the beauty of her body and the independence of her spirit in his work. Mallory, though young, has already suffered rejection because of the striking originality of his pieces, and is beginning to grow cynical regarding an innovative thinker's chances of gaining practical success. His relationship with Roark, however, inspires him. After his work on the Stoddard Temple, although still suffering from moments of despair, Mallory never again reaches the depths of torment he is in when Roark meets him. But Toohey, as was his plan, manipulates both Stoddard and the public. He denounces Roark's Temple as heretical, and society follows his lead, sending up a chorus of protests. The Stoddard Temple is torn down, and Roark is condemned as an apostate. Roark's career is now in a downturn in which he receives only a few very minor commissions.

Dominique, in agony at the attack on the hero she loves, marries Keating—the most despicable individual she can find—in an attempt to kill off in herself that greatness of soul that enables her to love only man at his highest and best. The destruction of the Stoddard Temple confirms Dominique's worst fears. It convinces her that she was right in wanting to avoid entanglement in a romantic relationship with Roark. His creative work and uncompromising character have no chance in a world that merely follows the beliefs it has been taught. He will be destroyed, just as Cameron was. This was, and remains, her deepest belief. Given her values, Dominique must love Roark and everything about the human potential that he represents. She loves man the noble hero. But society, in her view, leaves no place for such a hero's triumph. Therefore, the only choice, as Dominique sees it, is to kill off in herself her capacity for hero worship. In so doing, she can escape her agony when presented with the destruction of greatness. She believes that the way to kill in herself her capacity to respond to Roark is to thoroughly immerse herself in the life of Keating. The love of virtue and beauty, she hopes, cannot survive absorption into a life filled with corruption and ugliness. With full conscious intent, she marries Peter Keating.

Keating and Dominique are married for twenty months. Through Toohey's manipulation, Dominique is introduced to newspaper publisher Gail Wynand, for whose paper Dominique formerly worked as a columnist. The powerful Wynand is a man of mixed premises. Like Dominique, he worships man the noble hero, but, unlike her, he has sold his soul, publishing *The Banner*, a yellow-press scandal sheet, gaining him wealth and influence. Wynand, taken with Dominique's intelligence and idealism, as well as with her beauty, proposes marriage. Dominique, thinking she's found a man even lower than Keating, accepts; she divorces Keating and marries Wynand. The powerful publisher buys Keating's consent with a hefty check and the commission for Stoneridge Homes, a housing development he is building. But on her way to Reno to obtain the divorce, Dominique stops in the small town of Clayton, Ohio, where Roark is building a small department store. She has not seen him since her marriage to Keating. Roark notices from her questions that she is still concerned with other people and their ability to hurt—or even observe—him. She tells him that she wishes to remain with him in this small town. She says they can marry, that she will wash his clothes and cook his meals, and that he will give up architecture and work in a store. Out of consideration for her, he tries not to laugh. He tells her if he were cruel, he would accept her offer just to see how long it would take her to beg him to return to architecture. She understands. Roark knows that Dominique is not ready to stay with him. She boards the train for Reno and, after her divorce, marries Gail Wynand.

Wynand, though a man who panders to the masses in his professional life, privately worships only man's noblest achievements. Holding the same basic premises as Dominique, it is logical that he loves her. He becomes fanatically jealous of sharing Dominique with others. Wynand wishes to build a home in the country as an isolated fortress, so he will not have to see Dominique among the people of the city. Every time Wynand has seen a building he's admired, the architect has always been Howard Roark. So Wynand hires Roark to build his home. Wynand greatly admires both Roark's integrity and his genius, and he uses his great influence to bring to Roark a number of commissions. Roark's prominent buildings in New York City slowly begin to attract a growing number of individuals who understand the revolutionary nature of his designs. Roark receives more commissions and becomes better known.

One of the more prominent commissions he receives prior to his relationship with Wynand is for the Monadnock Valley Resort. The owners of the resort conceive it as a swindle. They sell two hundred percent of it. They are certain it will fail. They want it to fail. They choose Roark as the worst architect they can find. They believe that Roark's plan for separate houses where people can enjoy privacy, rather than be clustered together in one huge ant colony of a hotel, is an antisocial scheme bound to fail. They hire him because of it. But Roark's idea satisfies a need for a resort that was not currently met—and his design is spectacularly beautiful. People come, and the resort is successful. The owners are arrested for fraud, but Roark is not involved in the legal case. The simple fact, however, that Roark made money for people who did not want to make money impresses businessmen, and Roark receives commissions. Additionally, at the time of Monadnock's completion, Roark receives a telegram from Kent Lansing, now the legal owner of the Aquitania Hotel. Although Roark's original intent was to spend the first summer of Monadnock's existence at the resort, he now returns to New York City to complete the hotel.

The climax of *The Fountainhead* begins when Keating, whose career is slipping because he's been replaced by a newer trend, begs Roark to design for him plans for the new low-income housing project called Cortlandt Homes. Keating knows he cannot solve the problems of design, and does not attempt to. Instead, he brings the specifications to Roark. Keating requests that Roark design it and allow Keating to take the credit for it. Roark knows that he can do it and is eager to. He also knows that he could never get approved by Toohey, who is the behind-the-scenes power on the project. Roark agrees only on the condition that the buildings be erected exactly as he designs them; Keating agrees. Keating will receive the recognition, the money, and whatever other benefits society may confer on a man—but Roark will build Cortlandt. Roark designs a masterpiece, Keating submits it as his, and Toohey accepts it. But when Roark is away on a cruise with Wynand, two of Toohey's lackeys alter Roark's design. When Roark returns, he dynamites the defaced masterpiece and allows himself to be arrested. Significantly, he enlists Dominique's aid in the dynamiting. Whereas years earlier, she had been afraid that society would reject him, now she is not afraid to help Roark in an act for which society may imprison him. Roark knows that Dominique is now ready for their relationship.

Wynand embarks on a crusade to save Roark. Believing that his papers mold public opinion, Wynand defends Roark vociferously in *The Banner*. But Wynand's public does not care if a great genius has been wronged; they stop reading the paper in protest of Wynand's stance. When Wynand is out of town in a desperate attempt to save an advertising contract, Toohey strikes. Toohey, who writes a column for *The Banner*, has schemed for years to take over the paper. Gradually, he has maneuvered his followers into key editorial positions, and they all come out against Roark. When Wynand fires them, the union, controlled by Toohey, goes on strike. Wynand, with Dominique's help, struggles to get out the paper, but it comes back unread. To save the paper, Wynand is forced to reverse his stand on the Cortlandt dynamiting.

At his trial, Roark defends the right of the creator to the product of his effort. Roark points out that it was he who designed Cortlandt and that he was not paid for his work. The only price—that it be erected as designed—was not paid. He argues that an individual is not a slave to society, and that society has a claim to a creator's work only on his own terms. He points out that, down through the ages, creative men have often developed beneficial new ideas and products, only to be rejected by their societies. Despite social opposition, the creators move ahead, carrying the rest of mankind with them. Cortlandt Homes is the product of his mind; it is his creation and belongs to him. If society wants it—as it does—justice requires that his asking price be paid. It must be built as he designed it. The jury understands his position and votes to acquit him. Roger Enright buys Cortlandt Homes from the government and hires Roark to build it; Wynand, as long planned, hires Roark to build the Wynand Building, the tallest skyscraper in the city. Roark has achieved commercial success on his own terms.

The novel's climax brings to resolution the struggles of all five of the major characters. Roark sees his ideas finally winning in the field of architecture. After decades of the battle that he and Cameron fought, their new methods are ultimately gaining recognition. Dominique, seeing that she was mistaken in believing that a genius like Roark has no chance in a corrupt world, is liberated from her fears and is finally free to marry him. Wynand is psychologically and morally crushed by the realization that success did not require him to sell his soul to the masses, that his professional life was founded on a lie. When Toohey emerges victorious from the strike, prepared to dictate editorial policy on *The Banner*, Wynand shuts down the paper rather than allow Toohey to control it. Years of Toohey's scheming are wasted; he has failed both in his attempt to stop Roark and in his attempt to take over the Wynand papers. Toohey must start over at another paper, but time, for him, is running out—as it has for Keating, who is publicly exposed as a fraud at Roark's trial, as a man who puts his name on another man's work. Keating, who once enjoyed acclaim, now finds that his career in architecture is finished. He is a rotted-out shell of a man.

List of Characters

Howard Roark The hero of the story. It is his struggle to succeed as an architect on his own terms that forms the essence of the novel's conflict. His independent functioning serves as a standard by which to judge the other characters—either they are like Roark or they allow others, in one form or another, to control their lives. Roark is the embodiment of the great innovative thinkers who have carried mankind forward but are often opposed by their societies.

Henry Cameron Roark's mentor. He is an aged, bitter curmudgeon—and a commercial failure—but he is the greatest architect of his day. He is an early modernist, one of the first to design skyscrapers and a man of unbending integrity. Roark admires Cameron as he does no one else in the novel. His life exemplifies the fate of many innovators who have discovered new knowledge or invented a revolutionary product, only to be repudiated by society.

Dominique Francon An impassioned idealist who loves only man the hero. Dominique is Roark's lover, his greatest admirer, and, simultaneously, an ally of Roark's most implacable enemy—Ellsworth Toohey—in the attempt to ruin his career. Dominique, though a brilliant woman, holds a pessimistic philosophy throughout much of the novel that prevents her from fulfilling her vast potential.

Guy Francon Dominique's father. A phony architect, who achieves commercial success by two means: copying from the great classical designers, and wining and dining prospective clients with urbane wit and charm. His great financial success despite his unprincipled methods provides some of the evidence on which Dominique originally bases her conclusion that the world is essentially corrupt. Francon's tutelage helps Peter Keating develop into an even more unscrupulous manipulator than his boss.

Peter Keating The foil to Roark. He lacks the backbone to ever stand alone, and spends his life forever seeking the approval of others. He even codifies his toadying attitude into a formal principle: "Always be what people want you to be." Keating is an outstanding example of a status-seeking conformist.

Mrs. Louisa Keating Peter's mother. She seeks respectability above all. She teaches her son to put the values of others before his own. By encouraging her son to surrender his mind to others, she is indirectly responsible for causing his ultimate self-destruction.

Ellsworth Toohey Architectural critic and spiritual power broker. Toohey is simultaneously a cult leader acquiring a private army of slavish followers and a Marxist intellectual preaching socialism to the masses. Roark's refusal to obey threatens his hegemony in his own field, so he dedicates himself to Roark's destruction. The villain of the novel, Toohey represents collectivism in its most undiluted form.

Catherine Halsey Toohey's niece and Keating's fiancée. Catherine is an honest girl of only modest intellect and ambition, but she loves Peter sincerely. Keating's betrayal of her robs her of the only personal goal that she possesses and drives her to become one of her uncle's obedient followers.

Gail Wynand Powerful publisher of vulgar tabloids. Wynand combines a mixture of independent and dependent methods of functioning. In his personal life, he lives by his own judgment, but he panders shamelessly to the masses in his career. He is Roark's closest friend, yet the way he has sold his own principles to gain power is in sharp contrast to Roark's integrity. Wynand's life shows that it is impossible to attain happiness by embodying mutually exclusive premises.

Alvah Scarrett Wynand's chief editor. An unthinking "mom and apple pie" type of conservative, he is invaluable to Wynand as a means of gauging public opinion. Though loyal to Wynand, his abject conformity makes him easy prey for Toohey. He embodies the trite conventionality of popular culture.

Austen Heller Newspaper columnist who defends the rights of the individual. That he gives money generously to help political prisoners around the globe shows his respect for the independent mind. He gives Roark his first commission by hiring him to build a private home, then remains a trusted friend.

Steven Mallory Sculptor of significant ability, who portrays man the exalted hero in his figures. He sculpts the statue of Dominique for Roark's Temple of the Human Spirit. He, too, is a valued and loyal friend of Roark's.

Mike Donnigan Construction worker. He knows construction, scorns social opinion, and goes by his own judgment. A lifelong friend of Roark's, Mike's life shows that a person does not have to be a genius to be independent, but he must be willing to live by his own judgment.

Roger Enright Innovative businessman. He conceives a new idea for an apartment building—the Enright House—and hires Roark to build it. As a man who overturns previous thinking when entering a field, he is naturally attracted to Roark's revolutionary designs. Enright's life shows the independence necessary to be a successful entrepreneur.

Kent Lansing Member of the board set up to build the Aquitania Hotel, a luxury establishment on Central Park South. He battles for years, against a variety of obstacles, to get Roark hired and to complete the hotel's construction. Lansing is an example, as is Roark on a larger scale, of the unswerving dedication that an innovative thinker must possess if he is to reach his goals against a society opposed to change.

The Dean of Stanton Institute A traditionalist in architecture. His commitment to the established rules of design and unwillingness to consider new ideas make him the first of the many conformists with whom Roark comes into conflict. The Dean is more typical of Roark's antagonists than is the evil Toohey, for he is merely a social conservative, blind to the possibility and value of progress. Important for "the principle behind the Dean" that Roark seeks to understand.

Ralston Holcolmbe   Another traditionalist in architecture. Holcolmbe believes Renaissance is the only appropriate style of building for the modern world. He embodies a different type of conformity than Francon, who adheres to the Classical school of design. Both he and Francon are rigid dogmatists unwilling to consider the new ideas of modern architecture.

John Erik Snyte   An eclectic in the field of architecture. Snyte refuses to cling slavishly to one school of design; instead, he combines clashing styles into a hodgepodge of contradictory elements. As a man willing to give the public anything it wants, no matter how vulgar or inane, Snyte represents conformity in yet another form. In his own unprincipled way, it is his willingness to let Roark design in his own style that makes possible Roark's first commission.

Gordon L. Prescott   A phony architect who seeks to impress people by spouting the terminology of Hegelian dialectic. He is not concerned with building effectively, but merely with winning adulation from a gaping public. One of an army of nonconformists who conform utterly to Toohey's circle, Prescott is one of the characters illustrating that rebellious nonconformity is as slavish to the group as is blind conformity.

Gus Webb   One of Toohey's followers. An architect of the so-called "International Style," which rejects the blind following of traditional schools for barren, flat-topped structures devoid of any logical plan. A virulent nonconformist, rebelling against civility, personal hygiene, and all aspects of a rational life, Webb is a crude and vulgar lout, whose mindless activism on behalf of the "workers' revolution" contrasts with Toohey's cultured advocacy of Marxism. Whereas Toohey is representative of the intellectual "Old Left," Webb embodies the anti-intellectual, physical activism of the New Left.

Lois Cook   Another mindless rebel and follower of Toohey. She is an avant-garde writer who dispenses with coherent sentence structure. Lois Cook deliberately builds the "ugliest house" in New York and cultivates a slovenly appearance as means to shock the middle class. She and Gus Webb, in blindly rebelling against the values of society, are as controlled by other people as is an abject conformist like Keating.

Character Map

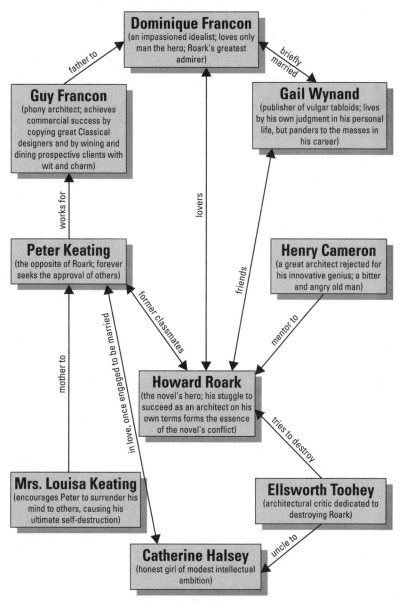

Dominique Francon (an impassioned idealist; loves only man the hero; Roark's greatest admirer)

Guy Francon (phony architect; achieves commercial success by copying great Classical designers and by wining and dining prospective clients with wit and charm)

father to

briefly married

Gail Wynand (publisher of vulgar tabloids; lives by his own judgment in his personal life, but panders to the masses in his career)

works for

lovers

Peter Keating (the opposite of Roark; forever seeks the approval of others)

Henry Cameron (a great architect rejected for his innovative genius; a bitter and angry old man)

friends

former classmates

mentor to

mother to

in love, once engaged to be married

Howard Roark (the novel's hero; his stuggle to succeed as an architect on his own terms forms the essence of the novel's conflict)

tries to destroy

Mrs. Louisa Keating (encourages Peter to surrender his mind to others, causing his ultimate self-destruction)

Ellsworth Toohey (architectural critic dedicated to destroying Roark)

Catherine Halsey (honest girl of modest intellectual ambition)

uncle to

CRITICAL COMMENTARIES

Part One
Peter Keating

Summary

As the novel opens, the hero, Howard Roark, has just been expelled for insubordination from the Architectural School of the Stanton Institute of Technology. Roark's designs are radically new, never before seen in the field of architecture, "sketches of buildings such as had never stood on the face of the earth." The Dean and members of the faculty are advocates of traditional designs; they want Roark to build in accordance with the established styles of the past. Roark, however, is a modernist designer and a man who thinks for himself. He does not accept the Dean's belief that the rules of architecture come from the thinkers of the past and should, therefore, be uncritically followed by modern designers. He tells the Dean that, in his judgment, there are three rules of design—the building's material, its site, and its purpose. All three rules necessitate an architect's rational assessment of the facts of a building's requirements; none of them can be applied by blind obedience to the work of the past.

Roark's independence extends to matters other than architecture. Even though he recognizes that the career path ahead of him will be arduous, he laughs at his expulsion from school. The school's action will make his future more difficult, but it cannot stop him. Roark's attitude is similar with strangers. People notice Howard Roark when he walks on the streets; he notices no one. In fact, he often arouses resentment in strangers, who somehow cannot explain what they feel when they see Roark. But Roark could walk the streets naked without concern; he has no regard for the evaluations of others.

Roark boards at the home of Mrs. Keating, whose son, Peter, graduates from Stanton with high honors on the same day that Roark is expelled. Keating is handsome, charming, and glib. He receives his high grades not by earning them, but by copying from the masters of the past, giving his teachers what they want and enlisting Roark's aid in solving structural problems. Keating is utterly dependent on others, and he is faced with a difficult decision. He has won a scholarship to the prestigious Ecole des Beaux-Arts in Paris. But he also has a job offer from Francon and Heyer, the leading architectural firm in the United States. Because either option will greatly impress people, he has no basis upon which to choose. He comes to Roark with the dilemma. Although he would never state it publicly, Keating realizes that Roark understands more of importance about architecture than do his professors, and that Roark loves the subject in a way that his professors do not. Privately, in his own conscience, Keating respects Roark's judgment more than he does the Dean's. Roark tells him that he has made a mistake, that he should not look to others for guidance regarding the decisions of his own life. He tells Keating that an individual must know what he wants in life. Their conversation is interrupted by the arrival of Mrs. Keating, who makes it clear that she does not want her son in Paris, an ocean away. The decision is made for him: He will go to New York to work for Francon and Heyer.

Roark and Keating pursue separate careers in architecture in New York City. Keating works for Guy Francon, a mediocre architect but a man who is possessed of all the social graces. Francon is the country's most successful and prestigious architect because of two qualities: He designs in the Classical style, giving the public the traditional buildings it is used to, and he wines and dines prospective clients at New York's most exclusive restaurants. Francon knows little about building, but a great deal about matching his ties with his handkerchiefs and his wines with his foods. He does not gain clients by the brilliance of his designs, but by the phony warmth of his smile. From Francon, Keating learns how to impress others, not how to build.

Keating has a girlfriend named Catherine Halsey, whom he met a year before in Boston, where she lived with her mother. She is plain and awkward with "nothing to her credit, but her lovely smile." Keating has dated the most beautiful, well-dressed girls, but it is the shy Katie that he prefers. Even though he forgets to call her for weeks at a time, Katie waits patiently for his attention. In the time since Keating met Katie, her mother has passed away and she now lives with her uncle in New York. Despite her proximity, he visits her only infrequently. But when he does, her sincerity compels him into an honesty that he exhibits nowhere else. When he finds that her uncle is Ellsworth Toohey, the rising star of architectural criticism, he tells her that, though he badly wants to meet Toohey, he will not do it through her. He makes an exception to his normal pattern of behavior when he is with Katie. Peter is disturbed to discover that Katie, who once planned to attend college, is now undecided due to her uncle's opposition. Keating is concerned that her uncle is acquiring too much control over her life.

While Keating slides up the corporate ladder at Francon's, Roark works for Henry Cameron, a brilliant architect and a man of unswerving dedication to his principles. Because Cameron is one of the first to design skyscrapers, his buildings are revolutionary. He is ahead of his time, and his designs are rejected by the public. Now sixty-nine, Cameron is a commercial failure and a bitter alcoholic, but also a genius and a man of great artistic integrity. Roark learns from Cameron the one thing of value: how to build.

Cameron is an important secondary character in the story. In the 1880s, he was the most successful architect in the country, personally designing every structure that came from his office, and building as he pleased. Clients took what he gave them without complaint. Although Cameron's work was ahead of its time, he proceeded in the full confidence of his own genius. His buildings were different, but this difference was not enough to frighten anybody. Other architects, in deference to tradition, attempted every visual trick to make their buildings look small and conventional. But Henry Cameron dispensed with all horizontal devices and flaunted his structure's lean vertical lines, erecting the first skyscrapers, buildings proud of their height. By 1892, his radical new designs began to win support, but the following year saw the opening of the Columbian Exposition of Chicago, a major turning point in Cameron's career.

The Exposition was a glorification of Classical architecture. Its designers copied every style of the Greeks and Romans, and all subsequent schools of history, eschewing all originality. The American public gaped at the Exposition and, in its architectural ignorance, was impressed. The Exposition's influence lent fuel to people's willingness to continue with the traditional things they were used to and to avoid the new and untried. Cameron refused to work for such an undertaking and called it names that were unprintable. When potential clients came to him with requests for banks or office buildings designed as copies of Classical structures, he became enraged; and even went so far as to throw an inkstand at a distinguished banker who had asked for a railroad station in the form of the temple of Diana at Ephesus.

The effect of the Columbian Exposition was to close the door on Henry Cameron's future in American architecture. When design became a matter of merely copying Classical structures, there was no room for the bold originality of Cameron's work. By the time Roark meets him thirty years later, Cameron is an embittered, hard-drinking, commercial failure. But Roark reveres him because of his unbetrayed architectural vision and chooses to work for him, knowing that this is the one man who can teach him what he needs to learn. Roark learns from Cameron the means to develop his brilliant architectural ability. Keating, on the other hand, learns from Francon how to polish his method of pandering to others.

Keating rises in Francon's firm by duplicitous means. He manipulates fellow employees, fawns over his superiors, and helps cause the death of Lucius Heyer, Francon's elderly partner, who stands in his way. Heyer, although not an architect, is a partner in Francon's firm for one reason: He comes from a wealthy, old-money background and is connected to the socially elite families who form the nucleus of Francon's client base. Because he is elderly, senile, and lonely, Heyer is generally treated with scorn at Francon's office. But Keating, realizing the value of a partner's patronage, fawns over the old man from his first day in the office. Because the only passion in Heyer's life is his porcelain collection, Keating studies the subject as a means of ingratiating himself with Francon's partner. After several years of meteoric rise, Keating is the firm's chief designer and ready for more. He looks to be Francon's partner, but Heyer blocks his path. Heyer has suffered a stroke and the doctors fear for his life. But his partnership in the firm gives his life meaning, and he stubbornly refuses to retire. Keating has reasons to want Heyer out of his way immediately. Francon believes in Keating and is confident that he will win the Cosmo-Slotnick competition. But despite the brilliance of Roark's plan, Keating believes he has no chance. He knows that the classical elements he has added to the design clash with the modernist nature of Roark's original; Keating is sure that his final result is a mongrelized mixture of contradictory styles, with no chance of winning. He must gain the partnership in Francon's firm before he loses the competition, while he still has Francon's trust. Keating, therefore, looks for a weapon he can use against Heyer. He discovers the slightest possibility of financial wrongdoing on Heyer's part, evidence too flimsy to stand up in court but perhaps sufficient in dealing with a sick old man. In private, he berates Heyer, verbally abusing him and demanding that he retire. The senile Heyer is puzzled and frightened that this friendly young man is screaming at him. The strain for Heyer is too much. He suffers the second stroke the doctors had feared and dies immediately. Keating, who calls for assistance in vain, receives sympathy at Francon's office, where he is perceived as the only friend Heyer had. He also receives a large inheritance from Heyer, who had no family. As the novel's first part concludes, Keating gains both the partnership he coveted and the wealth of Lucius Heyer's estate. He is, by conventional standards, an extremely successful man.

Keating's method of climbing the corporate ladder shows much about his character. A minor draftsman at the outset of his employment, his focus is not to improve his skills and rise through merit, but to exploit the weaknesses of his fellow employees and thereby remove them from his path. He discovers that Tim Davis is Francon's chief draftsman, and that Davis is engaged to be married. Keating ingratiates himself with Davis, seeking the more experienced man's trust. When Davis, who is apartment-hunting and planning his wedding, must be absent from work, Keating volunteers his assistance. He begins to do Davis' work when the older man must be away from the office. Over time, this becomes a permanent arrangement. Eventually, Francon notices that Keating is doing Davis' work and fires Davis, hiring Keating in his place. This was Keating's intention all along.

Claude Stengel is Francon's chief designer, doing all of the firm's creative work and getting none of the credit. His position is Keating's next step on the ladder. But Stengel is more perceptive than Davis and recognizes Keating's manipulative methods, rebuffing Keating's attempts at friendship. Stengel is ready to go out on his own and start his own firm; he just needs someone to give him his first commission. Keating understands the situation. By now, he has proven to be an apt pupil of Francon, charming prospective clients with suave urbanity. Francon puts him in charge of a potential account, expecting that Keating will deliver it to the firm. Instead, Keating surreptitiously convinces the client to hire Stengel. When Stengel takes the commission and departs, Francon is outraged at the perceived betrayal by Stengel, but does not suspect Keating, who slips into Stengel's vacated post.

At this point, Keating has created a problem for himself. Up until now his work has been limited to drafting—a sophisticated form of copying—of which he is eminently capable. But now he must design, producing creative work. At this, he is a failure. But Keating knows someone who is a superb designer. He brings the specifications for his first building to Roark, who helped him similarly with his college projects. Roark solves the building's structural problems and creates its plan. This arrangement establishes a pattern in the professional relationship of the two men: Roark often assists Keating with problems of design. Through Roark's help, Keating wins the Cosmo-Slotnick competition, a contest to design the "world's most beautiful building." At the end of Part One, though barely thirty, Keating is famous and a partner in the country's most prestigious firm.

Roark, by contrast, struggles. He endures poverty at Cameron's and faces rejection out on his own after the older man's retirement. Despite

Cameron's genius, chances at commissions dribble only slowly into his office, and most do not materialize. Cameron does not have the money to pay either rent or salaries, but Roark remains. Their one hope is the potential commission for the Securities Trust Company building. Cameron and Roark work night after night, with a pot of black coffee to keep them awake. On the last day of their vigil, Cameron is on the verge of collapse. Roark orders him home after midnight. The next day, when Cameron enters the office, he finds Roark fast asleep on the floor. The drawings, finished, are on the table. But the board of directors awards the commission to another firm of Gould and Pettingill. Cameron is left with a check that does not cover the cost of preparing his drawings and an electric bill that he cannot pay.

In the last two years of Roark's employment, Cameron begins to disappear for weeks at a time. Roark cannot find him at home, but knows he is off on a drinking binge and waits, hoping for the older man's safe return. Eventually, Cameron loses the shame of his drunkenness and staggers into his office, openly drunk in the one place on earth he had always revered. But, still, Cameron and Roark fight on; they keep the office open though the commissions are merely drops from a pipe that is slowly running dry. They take what they can get—country cottages, garages, remodeling of old buildings. But then the flow stops completely. When Cameron finally collapses, Roark takes him home. The doctor he summons tells them that an attempt to leave his bed will be enough to kill Cameron. Roark closes the office, and Cameron goes to live with an elderly sister in New Jersey.

Though Cameron offers Roark a letter of recommendation, Roark refuses to accept it, telling the older man, "You're not going to ask them for anything. Don't worry about me." But Roark struggles. There are few opportunities for an architect with radically new ideas. Peter Keating gets him a job at Francon's, where he can give Roark orders and use him as an errand boy, but Francon fires him when Roark seeks to design in his own manner, rather than in the Classical style that Francon requires. Finally, Roark gets a job with the architect, John Erik Snyte, who employs an unusual method of design. Snyte is an eclectic, who hires specialists in several historical styles; he has a Renaissance designer and a Gothic specialist, among others. He hires Roark to be his Modernist. Snyte permits each of his men to design in their own style, then melds the plans together into a final product. Therefore, Roark has the freedom to design as he likes, but his buildings will not be erected as he designs them. When the newspaper columnist, Austen Heller, comes to Snyte, desiring to build a private home, life changes for Roark.

Heller is an individualist who refuses to contribute to charity but who spends generous sums to help free political prisoners around the globe. He repudiates the clashing hodgepodge that Snyte offers, but recognizes great potential in the drawing. When Roark presents his original plan, Heller immediately responds and hires him on the spot. Roark builds the Heller house in Connecticut, his first commission in private practice; he opens his own office. Though there are those who, like Heller, recognize the brilliance of Roark's designs and hire him, they are rare individuals. Most men choose the safe and the known, that with which they have been surrounded all their lives. Roark receives a mere three commissions after the Heller house. The first comes from Jimmy Gowan, an auto mechanic who, after fifteen years of hard work, is ready to go out on his own and open a service station. Gowan has seen the Heller house, and though most people don't know what to make of the building, he likes what he sees. Gowan hires Roark to build his gas station.

At the end of Part One, the difference in the respective fortunes of Keating and Roark is striking: Keating celebrates his ascension to partnership in the country's most popular firm, whereas the penniless Roark is on his way to a granite quarry.

Other plot elements are introduced in this section. Mrs. Keating opposes her son's engagement to Catherine Halsey and insists that he woo Dominique Francon. Dominique is the boss's daughter, and Guy Francon practically begs Peter to establish a relationship with her. How will it look, Mrs. Keating asks Peter, if he prefers Katie to Dominique? It will insult Guy Francon and cost Peter a chance at the partnership. Additionally, Mrs. Keating stresses the importance of choosing the right wife for a successful career. Because Katie is plain and dull, she impresses no one. But Dominique's beauty and poised elegance command the respectful attention of everyone she meets. Peter cannot rise into the rarified air of high society with a vulgar little guttersnipe for a wife. His success requires a high-class woman at his side.

In keeping with the wishes of both his mother and his boss, and despite his love for Katie, Peter proposes marriage to Dominique Francon. Dominique is beautiful, elegant, and haughty—everything Katie is not. A brilliant, free-spirited, outspoken woman, Dominique sees with her own eyes and understands with her own mind. She recognizes that Keating is a manipulative fraud and says so to his face. She responds to his proposal with the remark that if she ever wishes to punish herself for some terrible misdeed, she will marry Keating. Keating proposes for the same reason he becomes an architect in the first place—because Dominique's poise, grace, and beauty will impress others in a way that Katie never could.

Dominique writes a column, "Your House," for *The New York Banner*, devoted to architectural design and interior decorating. *The Banner* is a lowbrow, yellow-press tabloid, specializing in a combination of lurid and overly-sentimental stories aimed at those with the most vulgar tastes. The paper is owned by Gail Wynand, a brilliant man of consummate artistic judgment, but one who panders ceaselessly to the lowest tastes of the crowd in order to gain wealth and political influence. (This ambivalent quality in Wynand's character has great impact on later events of the story.) Henry Cameron, on his deathbed, warns Roark of the dangers represented by the Wynand papers and by the factors in human nature that make them possible.

At the end of Part One, Rand has introduced the five major characters of the book—Howard Roark, Dominique Francon, Gail Wynand, Peter Keating, and Ellsworth Toohey—although most of the characters have not yet met one another. As the conflict develops, the meeting of the characters occurs in subsequent chapters.

Commentary

The conflict of *The Fountainhead* is presented immediately. The Dean of Stanton Institute believes that all great architecture has been done already by the masters of the past. The rules of design come from them; all that modern architects can do is copy. The Dean believes that truth is found in the beliefs of others and that an individual should follow the established route rather than forge a new path. The Dean is a *conformist.*

Character Insight

Peter Keating is a conformist even more fully than the Dean. He, too, copies from past architects. In addition, Keating grovels before all superiors, agreeing with them in order to win approval. He uses people, leeches off of Roark's work, and characteristically seeks to meet the expectations of others. He even chose architecture rather than the field he loves—painting—only to satisfy his mother. "Always be what people want you to be," he tells Roark, codifying his toadying policy into a principle. Keating is a man who refuses to think for himself; he follows, he copies, he obeys. He is utterly dependent on others for his convictions. He permits his life to be dominated by them.

Character Insight

Roark, however, thinks for himself—indeed, part of the book's meaning is that this phrase is a redundancy. If one thinks, it is necessarily by and for oneself; there is no other way to do it. Roark believes that architecture is a *creative* field, that it is important to innovate, and that new ideas have far greater value than copies of old ones. His defense of the freethinking mind is eloquent and to the point: "Why is it so important—what others have done? Why does it become sacred by the mere fact of not being your own? Why is anyone and everyone right so long as it's not yourself? Why does the number of those others take the place of truth? Why is truth made a mere matter of arithmetic—and only of addition at that?"

Roark upholds independence—the importance of a man thinking and acting for himself; in opposition to dependence—any form of an individual allowing his thought and life to be controlled by others. The essence of the book is the contrast and conflict between those who are independent and those who are dependent.

Literary Device

The conflict between the dependent and the independent takes place in different forms. One such form is the struggle between an innovator and the entrenched beliefs of a conservative society. Cameron and Roark have new ideas in architecture. They seek to build skyscrapers in an era when people have seen only two-story frame houses; they want to build with such new materials as glass, plastics, and light metals when people are accustomed only to wood and bricks. The battle Cameron and Roark fight against a society committed to following tradition is similar to the real-life struggle of such innovative modern designers as Louis Sullivan and Frank Lloyd Wright.

But Ayn Rand's thesis applies more broadly to the world rather than simply to architecture. History abounds with examples of great thinkers with brilliant new ideas who were opposed by the very societies that most benefited from them. Socrates was executed for the "crime" of philosophizing. Giordano Bruno was burned at the stake and Galileo threatened with torture for defending the heliocentric worldview in opposition to the geocentric view held by the Catholic Church. Darwin was attacked by religious Fundamentalists for his theory of evolution, and Scopes was jailed in Tennessee for teaching it. Inventors and discoverers of knowledge like Robert Fulton, Louis Pasteur, and the Wright brothers were denounced and their inventions rejected by many. Roark says, in his climactic courtroom address, that: "Throughout the centuries there were men who took first steps down new roads armed with nothing but their own vision. . . . The great creators—the thinkers, the artists, the scientists, the inventors—stood alone against the men of their time. . . . But the men of unborrowed vision went ahead. They fought, they suffered, and they paid. But they won." At this level of meaning, *The Fountainhead* is an impassioned defense of the innovator against the tradition-bound society that rejects him.

Style & Language

The word *fountainhead* means original source, as in the fountainhead of a river. Expressed in one form, the theme of the book is that the independent, reasoning mind is the original source of all human progress and prosperity. It is only men with new ideas who discover a way to make weapons for hunting, who discover ways to grow crops and domesticate livestock, who build the first homes and cities. The men who follow established ideas aren't the ones who invent automobiles, electric lighting systems, or airplanes. It is not the social followers who cure lethal diseases; it is only men of independent judgment.

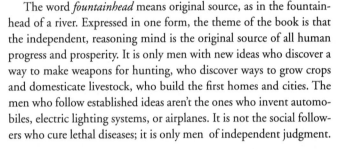
Theme

The novel's theme is implemented in other ways as well. One important way in which the theme of *The Fountainhead* is expressed involves a new understanding of the false alternative between conformity and nonconformity. A conformist is one who lives with blind acceptance of the convictions and values of others. The beliefs of other people serve as his standard of truth. The conformist's attitude is: "If you hold this to be true, then I believe it." He does not possess the courage to base his choices on his own thinking; instead, truth is social to him. The conformist permits the dominant beliefs of his family or society to control him, and he exists as a follower. The conformist refuses to use his mind, abdicating the responsibility of thinking and uncritically acquiescing to the opinions of others. The Dean and Peter Keating are examples of conformity. Guy Francon (who adheres rigidly to the Classical style), Ralston Holcolmbe (who copies Renaissance designs), and John Erik Snyte (who panders to the public taste) are also examples of conformists in *The Fountainhead*. Real life gives us a multitude of examples of conformists: the family who, "wanting to keep up with the Joneses," buys a new car or swimming pool because the neighbors have one; the teenager who knows drugs are dangerous but uses them anyway in order to gain acceptance from the peer group; the politician who surrenders his convictions because public opinion polls show they are unpopular; the student who aspires to study literature (or some other subject he loves) but gives it up because his family pressures him into medicine (or some other field it deems more appropriate). All of these, and numerous others, are conformists. The form in each case is different, but the essence remains the same. They all choose to follow others rather than be guided by their own judgment.

A commonly held belief is that the antithesis of a conformist is a *nonconformist*, but this is not the case. A nonconformist, too, allows others to dominate his life; that dominance merely takes a different form. A nonconformist lives in rebellion against the convictions and values of others. His attitude is: "If you hold this to be true, then I reject it." The fundamental issue remains the same. The nonconformist, too, refuses to use his mind. He also abdicates the responsibility of thinking; instead, he uncritically rebels against the opinions of others. For him, as well as for the conformist, truth is social: In the nonconformist's case, truth is the opposite of what his family or society believes. A nonconformist's starting point of knowledge is the beliefs of others; this is the ruling concern of his life. A good example of a nonconformist in *The Fountainhead* is Lois Cook, the avant-garde writer who rebels against the rules of grammar in her writing and against the rules of personal hygiene in her grooming. Real-life examples are those modern artists who rebel against beauty by deliberately making their works as ugly as possible, and the hippies of the 1960s who lived in rebellious opposition to the values of their middle-class families. A nonconformist is a variation on the same theme as the conformist: Both seek fundamentally to identify the beliefs of others—the conformist to obey, the nonconformist to rebel. Neither is concerned with living by the judgment of his own mind.

But Howard Roark is neither a follower nor a rebel. He is an individualist, a man who relies on his own thinking to form his own conclusions. Such an independent person is not concerned with what others think—neither to obey nor to defy them; rather, he is concerned with what he thinks. History abounds with innovators who are perfect examples: Copernicus, Columbus, Edison, and others were creative thinkers, discoverers of new knowledge, not men taking public opinion polls, concerned with ascertaining the beliefs of society and acting based on the results.

Conformists like Keating and nonconformists like Lois Cook are cognitive dependents, relying on others for their grasp of truth. Individualists like Roark are cognitively independent; instead of looking to society for truth, they look at the facts. Independent thinkers understand that truth is a relationship between an idea and reality, not a relationship between an idea and the number of its devotees. The Roarks of the world recognize that if many people hold an idea, that makes the idea popular but not necessarily true. Millions of people, perhaps all of human society, once believed the earth is flat—but, as we know today, they were mistaken. Truth is objective; it is not collective or inter-subjective. An independent thinker's devotion to the facts, not to the opinions of society, is what explains his ability to stand alone, often in the face of vehement antagonism. The conventional understanding that people are either conformists or nonconformists is inadequate. It overlooks the category of mankind's best members: the independent thinkers.

The independent man's unbreached commitment to the facts is shown in another important way. In response to the Dean's claim that the rules of design come from the architects of the past, Roark states his thinking on the subject. "'Rules?' said Roark. 'Here are my rules: what can be done with one substance must never be done with another. No two materials are alike. No two sites on earth are alike. No two buildings have the same purpose. The purpose, the site, the material determine the shape.'"

Roark's first rule addresses the material out of which the building will be made. Each material has a definite nature, a specific physical makeup that enables it to do certain things but prohibits it from doing others. Wood, for example, is suitable for a single-story home or other types of small structures, but is inadequate for skyscrapers or suspension bridges. Steel and concrete, on the other hand, can be used for such purposes; their molecular structures are such that they can withstand the necessary stresses. Roark's point is that advancing technology creates new materials that never before existed. Such substances as steel, aluminum, plastics, and glass were unavailable to earlier architects and make possible new types of designs. What is the logic, Roark asks, of copying the limited forms that were appropriate to wood when the new substances make possible so much more?

Roark's second rule concerns the site. An architect must know the facts of the area on which he builds. The consequence of not doing so is best exemplified by a New York neighborhood built on a filled-in swampland. The architects did not take into consideration the marshy nature of the terrain; their foundations were neither deep nor sufficiently strong; the result has been a gradual sinking into the ooze. Today, the houses rest below the level of the street. A positive example of Roark's point are those builders in San Francisco (on the San Andreas fault line) who construct their foundations on giant rollers, so that in case of earthquake the building can move in the direction of the earth's shifting tectonic plates. This is an example of knowing the site. Copying designs of the past, Roark points out, does not address these issues.

Finally, Roark's third rule concerns the purpose of the building, its function. Roark argues that no two buildings share the same purpose. "An airline terminal does not serve the same purpose as the Parthenon." Form follows function, according to the modernist designers, which means that every feature of a building—down to the placement of the last light fixture and doorknob—must be designed to maximize the building's purpose. A hospital, for example, deals with life-and-death emergencies. It requires wider corridors than most buildings so that the gurneys bearing the severely ill do not get clogged in pedestrian traffic. Again, the copying of prior designs would be inappropriate. The building's nature must dictate its design. Roark argues repeatedly that "a building has integrity, like a man." This is what he means. Integrity is to be true to oneself. A building must be a consistent whole, with every part designed to optimize its capacity to perform its function.

The independent thinker is like a scientist; he looks to nature, to the facts of reality, for truth. By contrast, a dependent person is like an unprincipled politician, looking to society, taking public opinion polls, in order to discover what he thinks is true. The dependent man and the independent man have differing concepts of truth; so the independent man is enabled to create new knowledge, whereas the dependent man is limited to merely copying the beliefs of others.

Ayn Rand provides an illustration of an independent man's method of functioning at the end of Roark's meeting with the Dean. Roark leaves the building knowing that there is an important difference between his way of thinking and the Dean's. He knows the motivation of persons like himself; he does not understand men like the Dean. "There was an important secret involved somewhere in that question, he thought. There was a principle which he must discover." Roark knows there are many persons like the Dean in society, and that he must learn to effectively deal with them. But when he steps outside, he stops. He sees the sunlight on the gray limestone of a stringcourse running along the wall of the building: "He forgot men, the Dean and the principle behind the Dean, which he wanted to discover. He thought only of how lovely the stone looked in the fragile light and of what he could have done with that stone." Roark sees in his mind walls of limestone rising, cut by bands of glass permitting the rays of the sun to become part of the classroom.

Theme

Roark's distinctive orientation is toward the stone and the sunlight, toward nature, toward facts, toward reality—and toward the structures he could build. He is not oriented toward society, toward men, or toward the beliefs of men. Though society and those who are a part of it are important—Roark must learn how to live with them—they fade to insignificance when he is faced with nature and her possibilities. Roark's method of functioning is that which makes possible human survival. To build, to grow, to create require human beings to deal directly with the laws and facts of reality. The beliefs, opinions, and errors of society are an enormously secondary consideration. This theme is more-fully developed in the novel's subsequent sections.

Glossary

(Here and in the following sections, difficult words and phrases, as well as allusions and historical references, are explained.)

frieze a sculptured or richly ornamented band on a building in classical architecture that is horizontal and rests on a column.

cornice a molded and projecting horizontal component at the top of a building.

volute a spiral, scroll-shaped ornament in Ionic and Corinthian architecture.

pediment a triangular space forming the gable of a low-pitched roof in Classical architecture.

pilaster an upright architectural member that is rectangular in shape and, though functionally a pier, serves primarily as a decoration.

facade the front of a building.

flying buttress a projecting structure arched over at the top to engage with a main wall. An important feature of Gothic architecture, lending strength to the main structure.

The Three Orders the schools of design in classical Greek architecture. These are the Doric, Ionic, and Corinthian. The Doric was the most basic and least ornate, and was used by the Spartans. The Ionic consisted of higher and slenderer columns. The Corinthian was more ornate, more detail-oriented, and not as widely used as the other two.

Gothic a style of architecture dominant in western Europe from the mid-twelfth century to the early-sixteenth century.

Part Two
Ellsworth Toohey

Summary

As Part Two begins, Howard Roark has closed his office and is working in a granite quarry owned by Guy Francon in Connecticut. Dominique Francon vacations that summer at her father's nearby estate. Visiting the quarry, Dominique meets Roark. Stirred by the taut lines of Roark's body, the proud, scornful demeanor of his face, Dominique pursues him. She comes to the quarry, where the workers engage in inhuman toil in the terrible heat. She wears a dress the color of water, a pale green-blue that flaunts the coolness of the gardens and drawing rooms from which she comes. She stresses her beauty and her name to Roark, the red-headed worker who stares at her insolently. His look says that he not only has the right to stare at her with arrogance and unspoken intimacy, but that she has given him that right. Dominique is angry but terrified that she has no control over the feelings this nameless worker arouses in her. She returns repeatedly to the quarry. Roark, despite being tired from the unspeakably hard labor, is attracted to this haughty and beautiful young woman.

Dominique, attempting to break the power she feels Roark has over her, stays away from him. But the safety of her home lacks the tense excitement he gives her; she flails at the white marble fireplace in her bedroom with a hammer and succeeds in scratching it; then she demands that he fix it. Roark looks at it, realizes what she has done, and breaks it with one blow of his hammer. "Now it's broken and has to be replaced," he tells her. He has it taken out and orders a new piece of marble from Alabama. Dominique waits for the marble to come "with the feverish intensity of a sudden mania; she counted the days; she watched the rare trucks on the road beyond the lawn." When the stone arrives, she barely glances at it. She sends to the quarry for the red-headed worker to come and set it. But Roark sends another worker in his place, and Dominique is enraged. She crosses paths with him several days later while riding her horse. When she asks why he didn't set the stone, Roark replies that he thought it made no difference to her who set the stone—but obviously it does. She lashes him across the face with her riding crop and rides away.

Three days later, Dominique still has not seen Roark. She sits alone at her dressing table late at night. She presses her fingertips, wet with perfume, to her temples, seeking relief in the cold bite of the liquid on her skin. She thinks she should try to sleep. Dominique does not hear the sounds of footsteps outside, even though the French windows of her bedroom are open to the garden. She hears the footsteps only as they rise up the stairs to her terrace. She looks at the French windows; Roark enters. Dominique resists him physically, but Roark refuses to relent. Although her servants are nearby, she refuses to scream. She is not certain whether, in the first instant of feeling his skin against hers, she thrust her elbows at his throat trying to escape or "whether she lay still in his arms." This was "the thing she had thought about, had expected, had never known to be like this, could not have known because this . . . was the kind of rapture she had wanted." Their result-ing lovemaking is so passionate that "it was not part of living, but a thing one could not bear longer than a second." When Roark leaves, not a word has been spoken between them. Dominique feels that she must bathe. When she looks at herself in the bathroom mirror, she sees the purple bruises left on her body by his mouth and she moans: "She knew that she would not take a bath. She knew that she wanted to keep the feel of his body, the traces of his body on hers, knowing also what such a desire implied." Rather than wash away her lover's touch, she lays all night on the cold tiles of the bathroom floor. As for Roark, when Roger Enright recalls him to New York to design the Enright House, he thinks of Dominique even then. Architecture is no longer the sole mistress of his soul.

Roger Enright is a hard-bitten entrepreneur who began his working life as a coal miner in Pennsylvania. A self-made man, no one had helped him on his way to becoming a millionaire. That, he says, is why no one ever stood in his way. He never bought a share of stock or sold a share in any of his enterprises. He holds his fortune single-handed, "as sim-ply as if he carried all his cash in his pocket." He owns an oil business, a publishing house, a restaurant, a radio shop, a garage, and a refriger-ator-manufacturing plant. Before venturing into a field, he studies it for a long time, then acts as if he's never heard of any of the field's accepted wisdom. Enright's innovative ventures sometimes fail but often succeed, and he runs them all with the same ferocious energy, working twelve hours a day. Roark's work on the Enright House brings not only recognition but also more work.

Anthony Cord, a young Wall Street tycoon, hires him to design his first office building, a towering skyscraper in the heart of midtown

Manhattan. Also, Kent Lansing, a member of the board formed to build a luxury hotel on Central Park South, wants Roark to design the building. For various reasons, the board is skeptical. Most have never heard of Roark, some have personal connections to other architects, some are influenced by the opinions of family members or friends. Lansing fights indefatigably for Roark. When Roark asks him why he is fighting for him, Lansing replies, "Why are you a good architect? Because you have certain standards of what is good, and they're your own, and you stand by them." Similarly, Lansing continues, he too has standards regarding a good hotel, they're his own, and Roark is the man who can give him what he wants. The other members of the board are against him, he tells Roark. But he has a huge advantage: They don't know what they want. He does. After a month of Lansing's battle, Roark signs a contract to build the Aquitania Hotel.

As the Enright House is built, Austen Heller seeks to take Roark to a social gathering of architects, critics, and potential clients. He wants Roark to make contacts; specifically, he wants Roark to meet Joel Sutton, an admirer of Enright who considers hiring Roark. Heller tells Roark that he does not want to hear anything more about granite quarries for a long time. When Heller mentions that Dominique Francon will be there, Roark agrees to go. At the party, Dominique is stunned to discover that her workingman lover is the designer of the Enright House. As Heller introduces them, Roark observes Dominique's demeanor. "There was no expression on her face, not even an effort to avoid expression." Roark thinks that it is strange to see a face presenting a bone structure and an arrangement of muscles but no meaning, a face as a simple anatomical feature, like a shoulder or an arm, no longer a mirror of thoughts or emotions. He and Dominique engage in polite conversation, formally correct, giving no one a clue to their real relationship. At the party, Joel Sutton expresses interest in hiring Roark for an office building, but he is disappointed that Roark does not play badminton, his hobby. Sutton likes Roark—he likes everybody—but he is easily influenced by others.

Dominique writes about the Enright House in her column. She says that the building is "essentially insolent," and a "mockery to all the structures of the city and the men who built them." Few readers understand that she attacks Roark's building because it is too brilliant for the mediocrity of its surrounding. Most readers miss the extravagant praise she pours on the Enright House—as she intends. They recognize only that she attacks the building. Joel Sutton, who respects her opinion, is disturbed by her criticism of the Enright House. She invites him to lunch, where she convinces him to hire Peter Keating, not Roark. After taking the commission away from Roark, she comes to his apartment that evening; they make love. Dominique gives herself to him "in a surrender more violent than her struggle had been." This sets a pattern for their relationship: Dominique works by day to take commissions away from Roark—and at night she makes love to him.

Dominique joins forces with Ellsworth Toohey in an anti-Roark alliance. For differing reasons, they are determined to wreck Roark's career. They agree that both will work, each in their own way, to take commissions from Roark and bring them to Keating. To this end, Dominique uses her grace, beauty, and connections to throw dinner parties to which she invites prospective clients, and at which she charms them into hiring Keating. Under the guise of attacking Roark's buildings, she continues to praise them in print, until Toohey convinces her to stop advertising Roark's name in her column. Enright, who respects her, is angered by her comments regarding the Enright House. He takes her to the construction site, and is not surprised by her ecstatic reaction to the building. But he is puzzled to later read in her column such remarks as, "I wish that in some future air raid a bomb would blast this house out of existence. . . . So much better than to see it growing old and soot-stained, degraded by . . . the dirty socks and grapefruit rinds of its inhabitants. There is not a person in New York City who should be allowed to live in this building." Enright is not certain if she attacks the building because she doesn't like it or because she thinks it is so good that society does not deserve it. Roark understands her methods, as does Toohey. Dominique stops mentioning Roark and his buildings in her column.

Despite some successes, Toohey realizes that the anti-Roark campaign is failing. The Enright House, the Cord Building, and the Aquitania Hotel combine to give Roark a degree of publicity. Toohey is worried by Roark's growing recognition. He convinces a follower, Hopton Stoddard, to hire Roark to build a temple. Toohey knows that Roark's building will feature a magnificent but revolutionary design, one so original that he can then accuse Roark of attacking all of the accepted precepts of religion. Toohey is right regarding Roark's design—it is an architectural masterpiece. Further, Roark hires the brilliant young sculptor, Steven Mallory, to design the Temple's sculpture. Mallory, like Roark, has a vision of man the noble hero, capable of greatness. Mallory's figures reflect this respect for man. Because of the startling originality of his work, Mallory, though young, has already faced rejection in favor of more conventional sculptors. He is cynical and outraged at the injustices of society. He takes a shot at Ellsworth Toohey, because he believes that Toohey knows everything about the deeper causes of these injustices and supports them. When Roark meets him, he is drifting toward dissolution. He doesn't keep his appointment with Roark, he makes no contact to explain his absence, he is drunk when Roark meets him for the first time, and he is rude when Roark comes to his apartment. But Roark recognizes Mallory as both a great talent and a spiritual comrade. Roark hires Mallory, he encourages him, and Roark's example inspires the boy. Mallory's sculpture for the Stoddard Temple is worthy of the Temple itself. Another reason for its beauty is the fact that Dominique agrees to pose for the Temple's central sculpture. The three of them—architect, sculptor, model—are joined by Mike Donnigan, Roark's construction worker friend, in a bond similar to that felt by individuals on a crusade. They understand that the building of the Temple to the Human Spirit is a sacred undertaking.

But, in the end, Toohey's scheme succeeds in convincing the public that Roark is an enemy of religion. Toohey convinces Stoddard, who blindly follows him, to file a lawsuit against Roark. In the case and in the public furor that surrounds it, Toohey masterminds a concerted attack on Roark's building, claiming that, as a radical departure from every known principle of religious architecture, it represents an assault on all that has been traditionally held as holy. Most people accept Toohey's assessment, and Roark is now infamous. At the trial, Dominique, testifying for the prosecution, claims that Roark's Temple of the Human Spirit should be torn down because mankind is unwilling to live up to its exalted standard. Though testifying for the plaintiff, Dominique makes clear her appraisal that Roark designed a masterpiece of which society is unworthy. The Temple should be torn down, she argues, in order to save it from society.

Stoddard wins the case. After the trial, Dominique accepts Keating's earlier proposal of marriage. Keating goes ahead with the wedding immediately, despite being scheduled to marry Catherine Halsey, the girl he loves, the following morning. To make matters worse for Roark, construction is stopped on the Aquitania Hotel due to legal problems among the owners. Though Kent Lansing vows to gain legal control of the project and retain Roark to complete it, they both understand that the battles in court will take years to resolve. At the end of Part Two, Roark is once again at a low ebb: He is unable to get commissions, the few he does receive result in construction stoppage or worse, and the woman he loves has left him to marry his enemy. It appears that Ellsworth Toohey's schemes against him are destined to succeed in ruining his career.

Still, Toohey is unsure of himself. He needs from Roark some confirmation of his power, even if only Roark's admission that Toohey has succeeded in hurting him. He manufactures reasons to spend time at the renovated Stoddard Home for sickly children (the building once intended to be the Stoddard Temple), hoping to one day meet Roark there. When Roark does appear to examine the botch made of his design, Toohey waits for him. He asks Roark what he thinks of him. Roark answers in simple honesty that he does not think of him. Toohey understands that, though he has succeeded both in taking away commissions from Roark and in making his name notorious, he will never be able to touch Roark's independent spirit, which will go on designing revolutionary structures.

Commentary

Ellsworth Toohey's character is stressed in this section. Up until the construction of the Enright House, Toohey has had to take no action against Roark; the originality of Roark's designs was sufficient to keep a convention-following society from recognizing him. But at this stage of Roark's career, a series of independent men hire him for major projects. Roger Enright is the first. Enright, a tough and innovative entrepreneur, understands that Roark is the only choice for the new type of apartment building that he has in mind. This is the chance that Roark needs. The brilliance of his design attracts to him Anthony Cord (for the construction of an office building) and Kent Lansing (for the construction of a hotel).

Roark's success threatens Toohey. Toohey, a powerful critic, seeks control over the field of architecture as a means of gaining wider power. Roark's independence stands in the way of this control. He launches a multi-front campaign designed to stop Roark. First, he will not mention Roark in his column, even to attack him; he convinces Dominique to do the same, refusing to grant Roark free publicity. Further, he enlists Dominique's support and, together, they convince prospective clients to reject Roark and hire Keating, a jellyfish thoroughly under Toohey's control. Finally, when Roark succeeds despite these measures, Toohey conceives and executes the Stoddard Temple plan, a brilliant scheme of manipulation and character assassination. By the end of Part Two, Toohey's machinations have reduced Roark to the second and last nadir of his career; Toohey now stands at the high point of his power. In the book's final half, Toohey's ability to impede Roark's practical success is gradually reduced to naught.

The complex relationship of Roark and Dominique is further developed in this section. Though Dominique loves Roark with intense devotion, she willingly joins with Toohey in the attempt to destroy him. She does this because the reason she loves him clashes with her understanding of what is and is not possible in society. She loves Roark for the unbending independence of his spirit, the creative originality that designs revolutionary masterpieces. But she believes that society does not and will not value these innovations. Dominique looks at the career of her father, Guy Francon, and at the lives of Peter Keating, Henry Cameron, and Howard Roark. She sees that her father, a mediocre architect, charms his way to great success; that Keating, a manipulative fraud, uses deceit and flattery as a means to climb the corporate ladder; that Cameron, the world's greatest architect, ends as a drunken failure; and that Roark, the brilliant young designer, is forced to work in a quarry. She observes that Wynand's pandering leads to great success and, above all, she sees Ellsworth Toohey—whom she knows to be monstrously evil—embraced as a saint of virtue by society. Because of events like these, Dominique comes to the conclusion that men of integrity have no chance in human society, that only the most corrupt and evil will succeed. She thinks that Roark has no chance; that his genius and unbending integrity—the very qualities for which she loves and admires him—are the reasons for which he will be rejected. Watching the process by which greatness is destroyed by a crowd of envious mediocre people is agonizing for Dominique. She cannot bear to observe as society drives Roark to the same fate as Cameron. Because she believes that she is powerless to save Roark, her only recourse is to destroy him herself—not as the act of spiritual murder that Toohey seeks, but as an act of mercy killing. Roark must die by her hand, the hand of one who understands and loves him, not by the hand of an indifferent or corrupt society. This is her motivation in forming an anti-Roark alliance with Toohey. As Toohey observes, though their reasons may be different, they are working toward the same end.

Ellsworth Toohey has been a power seeker since childhood. He was a sickly and frail child, bitterly resentful of the healthier boys capable of excelling at physical contests. Instead of embarking on a constructive program of building his strength, Toohey chooses the destructive path of tearing down others. He seeks power over them in every possible way. Even as a child, he cultivates a following among the hapless and downtrodden. Under the guise of friendship and support, he takes over their souls, telling them how to conduct their lives. First he embraces Christianity; later, the socialist philosophy of Marx. Either way, he stands for one constant—the morality of self-sacrifice—for he intends to be the beneficiary of those sacrifices.

Toohey preaches a doctrine of selfless service to society. He is an altruist and collectivist. He believes that the group is more important than the individual, and that an individual exists solely to serve others, which stands in stark contrast to Roark's completely opposite views. Toohey is virulently opposed to the individualism of Roark, to the principle that an individual has "inalienable rights" and that a man has the right to live his own life. Toohey's values are those that underlie Communism and Nazism—the supremacy of the State or "the People" over the individual. Roark's values are those that underlie the original founding principles of the United States—the sovereign right of the individual. Roark's commitment to independent life stands in direct opposition to Toohey's goal of establishing a Communist or Fascist dictatorship in the United States. "Great men can't be ruled," Toohey states. "Therefore, we don't want any great men." Given the book's theme, this statement should be understood to mean, "Independent men can't be ruled. Therefore, we don't want any independent men."

Toohey's power-seeking activities are manifested in two interrelated forms. At the private level, he cultivates a legion of brainwashed followers who have relinquished all independent functioning and obey his every command. Toohey is a cult leader in this regard, exactly like such real-life figures as Jim Jones, David Koresh, and Sun Myung Moon. His method is to convince others to give up their values, those things they most love and that give their lives meaning. "No," he advises one boy. "I wouldn't go in for music if I were you. . . . That's just the trouble— that you love it. . . . Give it up. Yes, even if it hurts like hell." When a weak-minded person like Peter Keating gives up what he wants, his life is experienced as empty. He needs someone to fill it with purpose and meaning. He is no longer capable of doing this independently; he needs someone to do it externally. Ellsworth Toohey "was never too busy to give them his full attention," and he fills this void.

In the act of co-opting men's souls, Toohey is simultaneously furthering his political goals. A citizenry of independent thinkers, like Roark and Dominique, will not follow the commands of a Hitler or a Stalin. A society of independent men will form a political system of independence in which individuals are left free to pursue their own goals. A collectivist dictatorship requires a society of Peter Keatings, who are eager to obey a leader in exchange for approval and security. In the United States, Toohey faces a heritage of individualism and personal liberty that collectivists in Germany, Russia, or China would not. Toohey knows that every person he turns into a mindless zombie readies the country by just that much for the collectivist state he seeks. His followers will continue to obey if he is able to reach his goal of establishing a collectivist dictatorship in the United States with himself as chief intellectual advisor to the dictator.

Character Insight

Toohey is a man whose life is utterly dominated by other men— by the schemes, scams, plots, and machinations necessary to control others. Even Peter Keating, blind follower that he is, lives a more independent existence; for at least Keating can design buildings, however ineptly, and at least Keating can love a women, however tragically. But Toohey does not accomplish even this much. His entire existence is devoted to gaining spiritual and political power over others. Others are not merely the dominant—they are the exclusive—factor in his life. In this way, Toohey forms the sharpest contrast with Roark. Where Roark's life is devoted to nature (to gaining the knowledge and expertise necessary to build, to deal effectively with physical reality), Toohey's life is devoted to society (to identifying weaknesses in, and gaining mastery over, other men). Both men seek power—Roark over nature, Toohey over men. The contrast is presented brilliantly in the closing scene of Part Two. Toohey asks Roark what he thinks of him; Roark answers honestly, with no bravado, "I don't think of you." Toohey's existence is defined by what others think of him; they are his reality; he is real only in their evaluations. He needs others to regard him as an important (indeed, the all-important) factor in their lives. But this is not so for Roark. "Toohey looked at him, and then at the bare trees around them, at the river far below, at the great rise of the sky beyond the river." The trees, the river, the sky—the forces and life forms of nature—these are Roark's domain. Roark can deal effectively with nature; he can survive independently; he has no need to conquer or control others. On the contrary, he has that which conquerors seek to control—the capacity to build and grow, the ability to create abundance. In this moment, Toohey comes face-to-face with the stark contrast between himself and Roark. Toohey's face has the quality of "listening to something as simple as fate." At some unadmitted level of consciousness, Toohey has just realized the contrast between Roark and himself, and he sees now why this is a battle he cannot win.

Toohey has no chance with independent men who have no need of him. But with dependent souls, like his niece, Catherine Halsey, he has complete success. He preaches to her the evil of selfishness and the virtue of selflessness. But Katie loves Peter Keating sincerely. She realizes that selflessness entails the sacrifice of her values, including the renunciation of her engagement, and she recoils from this. At some uncomprehended emotional level, Katie senses her uncle's threat. When convinced that Keating will marry her, she spontaneously cries: "I'm not afraid of you, Uncle Ellsworth!" But Keating does not marry her. Toohey has long urged Keating to marry Dominique instead. When Toohey succeeds in this goal, he has accomplished two tasks with one stroke: He has emptied Keating's soul of its last personal value, and he has emptied Katie's soul of its only one. Both are now utterly selfless, devoid of loves of their own. Both are now floundering wrecks, whose empty lives are absent of meaning and who are incapable of self-guidance. Toohey, the spider ever increasing his supply of flies, has just added two more to his web. From now on, he controls the lives of both Keating and his niece. But he fails miserably with Roark.

Despite the notoriety of the Stoddard Temple—Toohey's best effort against Roark—the decline in Roark's career is only temporary. The Enright House, the Cord Building, the Aquitania Hotel, and the Stoddard Temple are major projects, and Roark's designs are brilliant. These buildings are known and will attract to Roark in the future the kind of clients who care only about the quality of an architect's work, and not about his social standing. Primarily, these buildings will draw Gail Wynand's attention to Roark's work—with significant positive consequences for Roark's career.

Roark's life is profoundly improved in another way, as well: his relationship with Dominique Francon. Dominique is intensely idealistic—she responds positively only to the sight of man's noblest accomplishments. Her reverence for the Greek statuette, for Roark's buildings, and for his character demonstrate her commitment to man at his highest and best. She can feel nothing, only indifference, for anything less. Dominique is a sincere hero-worshipper. She understands that the greatest men and women of history—Aristotle, Michelangelo, Leonardo da Vinci, Marie Curie—represent the human potential; she knows that these are the individuals we must admire and emulate. Dominique will settle for nothing less. Howard Roark is that ideal, and Dominique recognizes it instantly. Though consciously wondering at the quarry whether Roark is a convict, Dominique responds to Roark at a deeper level. Reminiscent of Aristotle's insight that "the eyes are the windows of the soul," she recognizes that Roark's "is the face of a god," as she later explains to Kiki Holcolmbe. It is important to note, regarding Dominique, that, despite meeting Roark at the lowest point of his career, she knows from one glance at his face, his eyes, his posture, his movements, that there is some special and proud quality about this man. Later, she is not surprised to discover that he is the designer of the Enright House. She gives herself to Roark in the first moment of meeting and, at the deepest spiritual level, remains true to him for the rest of her life.

But for all her idealism, Dominique is also a pessimist. She believes that the rare individuals and works of integrity she worships have no chance; that the world is corrupt; that phonies like her father and Peter Keating achieve success and acclaim, whereas geniuses like Henry Cameron and Howard Roark end up either as drunken failures or laborers in granite quarries. This is why, for a long time, Dominique does not oppose, and even aids, Toohey—for she believes that his evil is all the world deserves. It is also why she destroys the priceless Greek statuette that she worships—because the world it suggests does not exist. More importantly, it explains why Dominique resists Roark physically at the quarry and why, later, she joins with Toohey in an attempt to wreck his career. In her view, Roark, the proud man of integrity, will be destroyed by a society that fears and envies his greatness. If she allows herself to love him, then her pain at his destruction will be unbearable. But, given her values, Dominique cannot help but love Roark. Therefore, his inevitable destruction must come from the hand of one who understands and loves him—hers—not from the hand of a society that rejects him. Her alliance with Toohey seeks a common goal—Roark's destruction—but for opposite reasons. Toohey seeks spiritual murder, because Roark will not fit into the collectivist dictatorship Toohey hopes to establish; Dominique seeks mercy killing, so that the world cannot kill Roark slowly and agonizingly, as it did Cameron. Toohey looks to save his world from Roark; Dominique looks to save Roark from the world. They agree: Roark's career must die.

Roark loves Dominique for a deeper reason than her beauty and elegance, for something even rarer than her brilliant mind: Her idealistic devotion to the nobility of man matches his own. Despite her pessimism, her alliance with Toohey, and her marriage to Keating, the value that her love adds to Roark's life is incalculable. Roark now has a soul mate and lover who shares his deepest views of life and man. The depth of spiritual closeness they achieve is shown throughout the story, but one memorable scene stands out.

The Stoddard Temple is Dominique's worst fear realized. Roark designs a masterpiece that the world, in its evil and its ignorance, destroys. Her suffering is far worse than his. She comes to his room on the evening that Stoddard announces his lawsuit. She says nothing, but Roark knows at a glance what she feels, and that she feels it for him. "'You're wrong,' he said. They could always speak like this to each other, continuing a conversation they had not begun. His voice was gentle. 'I don't feel that.'" This dialogue between lovers illustrates that their intimacy is such that a wordless glance suffices to inform each of the other's deepest thoughts and emotions. Roark knows that despite Dominique's marriage to Keating, he will not lose her. They are bound to each other by deeper ties than a wedding vow.

Dominique marries Keating as an act of spiritual anesthesia. It is her idealism—her commitment to Roark and to all manifestations of human stature—that condemns her to suffering in a world that rejects her values. She seeks to kill off in herself (or at least put to sleep) her capacity to respond to sights of man's greatness. Keating is an unprincipled man, utterly devoid of the noble values that Dominique treasures. By immersing herself in Keating's life—by being a dutiful wife, by arranging his social calendar, by smiling at men of influence, by sleeping with him—she seeks to lose her attitude of man-worship. Dominique, a woman capable of loving only the equivalents of Michelangelo, in unbearable pain living in a world that repudiates such exalted standards, seeks to rid her spirit of its capacity for reverence by filling her life with the individual least deserving of it. But, as Nietzsche said, nobility of soul "is not to be lost." Dominique's quest is hopeless. Her reverence for man's greatness is the essence of her soul; it is ineradicable. This is the deepest reason that Roark cannot lose her.

Another development in Part Two is the introduction of Steven Mallory's character. When we meet him, Mallory is going a direction similar to that traveled by Henry Cameron. He is a brilliant young sculptor, whose work possesses "a magnificent respect for the human being." Roark chooses him to do the sculpture for the Stoddard Temple because his figures "are the heroic in man." But Mallory is tormented by the same evils that defeated Cameron and plague Dominique. His genius and originality are neither recognized nor valued. He is characteristically rejected by society in favor of sculptors who give the public works, not of man the hero but of trite conventionality. Mallory is already becoming bitter and cynical. He misses his appointment with Roark; he is drunk when Roark comes to his apartment; he is rude. But Roark recognizes him as an ally in his crusade. He encourages the boy; he shows him how much is possible; he hires him and, later, pays for his time so that Mallory can work as he wants. Most of all, by being the independent man he is, unconcerned with society's rejection, Roark inspires Mallory. Mallory was on his way to cynical dissolution, because he thought that the innovators have no chance. Roark shows him, in action, that they do. Mallory, like Cameron, is, in effect, a part of Roark's family. The elderly Cameron, Roark's teacher, is a father figure; the youthful Mallory, whom Roark mentors, is like a younger brother. Mallory's career will soon receive an upward boost from the same source as Roark's—the patronage of Gail Wynand.

Glossary

conformity an unthinking acceptance of the beliefs of other people. Here, it applies to a number of negative characters, especially Peter Keating.

nonconformity an unthinking rebellion against the beliefs of others. Here, it applies to negative characters, such as Lois Cook and Gus Webb.

individualism the theory claiming that an individual has certain "inalienable" rights (such as freedom of speech) that must not be violated by society. Here, the right of an individual to his own life is embodied in the character of Howard Roark.

collectivism the theory claiming that an individual exists solely to serve society, and that he possesses no right to his own life. Here, the theory is embodied in the character of Ellsworth Toohey.

innovator a person who has new ideas and, consequently, develops new methods and/or products. Here, it is represented by such heroes as Henry Cameron, Howard Roark, and Steven Mallory.

independence reliance on one's own thinking in the search for truth, rather than a blind acceptance of or rebellion against the thinking of others. Here, the character of Howard Roark is its fullest expression.

dependence permitting others to dominate one's beliefs, either in the form of following their thinking or rebelling against it. Here, this failure to function independently is, in one form or another, the hallmark of all the villains.

fountainhead the original source of something, such as a river. Here, it means that the independent reasoning mind is the original source of all human progress and prosperity.

compromise the vice of betraying those things most important to an individual, a violation of integrity. Here, shown in the life of Peter Keating.

idealism a commitment to man at his highest and best. Here, applicable to all of the heroes, most importantly Howard Roark and Dominique Francon.

pessimism the belief that the good have no chance to succeed in the world, that only the evil will flourish. Here, shown as a mistaken view held by Dominique Francon.

Part Three
Gail Wynand

Summary

Gail Wynand, contemplating suicide, looks back on his life, searching for a reason to live. He remembers growing up in the harsh slums of Hell's Kitchen, being the smart, tough leader of a street gang and being entirely self-educated. Wynand remembers the long, arduous struggle to start *The New York Banner* and to build its circulation; he thinks of the men he has ruined, the fortune he has made, the power he has attained—and of the way he has used his genius to pander to the lowest tastes of the crowd. The thought of death brings him no fear; the thought of life causes the fear of identifying his life's meaning. Wynand knows that he will not die now.

Ellsworth Toohey, for his own reasons, brings Wynand and Dominique together. Dominique has been married to Keating for almost two years. The marriage has helped Keating become the most successful architect in the country but has left Dominique utterly unaffected. Wynand, whose real estate empire exceeds his journalistic one, is planning a development—Stoneridge Homes. In the Depression, with building at a minimum, architects compete for the commission. Toohey, under the guise of seeking the commission for Keating, his protégé, brings about the introduction of Dominique to Wynand. Toohey's motives in this introduction involve his endless quest for power. Wynand is his major target, Dominique his minor. Toohey is scheming to take control of *The New York Banner*, to reach the day when he dictates editorial policy on New York's most popular newspaper. To this end, he worms his way into the confidence of Alvah Scarrett, Wynand's chief editor. He recommends candidates for jobs as they open up and gradually gets his followers onto Wynand's staff. He uses his influence to begin advocating his philosophy throughout the pages of *The Banner*. In various subtle forms, he has his followers push Lois Cook and her book, *The Gallant Gallstone*. His motives in this are typical. If he can get Lois Cook, his follower, to the top of the literary profession, then he not only acquires greater power over that important field, but he makes it much more difficult for an independent thinker to gain recognition. Just as Keating's ascension in architecture makes it more difficult for Roark to succeed, so Lois Cook's establishment will intensify the hardships for a Roark-like writer. If a fawning conformist like Keating is considered a great architect, then a bold innovator like Roark cannot be. Similarly, with Lois Cook and her antitheses in literature. When literary success requires posturing nonconformity, it leaves no room for a sincere man of genius. Further, the theme of Lois Cook's book is that individuals are powerless to control their own destinies, that they are at the mercy of some powerful outside force. This fits perfectly with Toohey's message that an individual is merely a cog in a vast social machine, and that each individual should voluntarily submit to society's commands.

The problem for Toohey is that Wynand is too observant. Despite the subtlety with which Toohey orchestrates the attempt to advertise *The Gallant Gallstone* on *The Banner*, Wynand notices his attempt and immediately puts an end to it. Toohey needs some means to distract Wynand, to shift his attention away from his paper and on to something else. Knowing Wynand's reputation as a womanizer, Toohey seeks to introduce him to Dominique. Toohey hopes that Wynand will be so captivated by Dominique's combination of beauty, charm, and intellect that he will get caught up in a relationship with her, thereby paying less attention to the details of his newspaper. This is the principal reason that he attempts to introduce them. He secretly purchases Mallory's statue of Dominique and gives it to Wynand as a gift. He believes that after Wynand sees it, he will be eager to meet the model.

Toohey also has a secondary purpose in bringing Dominique together with Wynand. He realizes that Dominique is a potentially dangerous antagonist. She is one of the few characters who understands that Toohey's real goal is the acquisition of spiritual and political power. Further, she regards such a destructive purpose as utterly evil. Toohey realizes that if Dominique ever changes her mind regarding the pessimistic philosophy she holds—if she comes to the conclusion that the world deserves better than the collectivist dictatorship that Toohey plans for it—then she will be able to take steps against him. With her brains, she will make a formidable adversary. Toohey would like to throw the deathblow of Dominique's soul. He understands both that she married Keating as an attempt to eradicate her attitude of hero worship, and that the attempt failed. Toohey hopes that a relationship with Gail Wynand—a man whose professional life is exclusively devoted to the most shameless pandering—will be able to accomplish what marriage to Peter Keating did not. If immersion in the corruption of Wynand's career can make Dominique indifferent to the sight of a hero, than she will not be outraged by Toohey's attempt to destroy all heroes. Her potential threat to him will thereby be removed. This is also one of his reasons for presenting Mallory's statue of Dominique to Wynand.

Wynand falls in love with Dominique. Her idealism—an ineradicable devotion to the highest achievements possible to man—is exceptional. Wynand, for all his pandering, retains in his soul a similar undying commitment to man at his noblest and best. He is drawn to Dominique for her best qualities. Dominique goes with Wynand for a cruise on his yacht, the *I Do*. He proposes marriage to her. Dominique, motivated by the same reason that impelled her to marry Keating, accepts. In effect, she marries more than a man, she marries *The New York Banner* and every tawdry value it stands for. She becomes "Mrs. Wynand Papers," and will seek to torment her husband for the cheap vulgarity of his journalism—and, above all, for his campaign against the Stoddard Temple.

When Dominique and Wynand return from the cruise, she is still married to Keating. Wynand buys Keating's consent to a divorce with a signed contract for the Stoneridge project and a check for a quarter of a million dollars. Keating, humiliated by his own lack of backbone, collects his group of friends and takes them out drinking. Keating is eager to pay for everything and gives exorbitant tips. As they consume the liquor, Keating asks repeatedly, "We're friends—aren't we friends?" His comrades nod in agreement. The blurred eyes looking back at him are soft and comforting.

Before leaving for Reno to obtain a divorce, Dominique visits Steven Mallory at his home. She has not seen Roark for twenty months. Once in a while during this period, she has called on Mallory. He understood that those rare evenings were moments in which she ached for a sight of her homeland, and that she could permit herself just a few of those moments. Entering Mallory's studio after a lengthy absence, Dominique observes the sudden prosperity reflected in his new possessions and realizes it is a result of Wynand's patronage—that Wynand, after examining the statue of Dominique, desired other works by the same sculptor and chose only the best. Though Mallory has purchased various new artworks, Dominique observes that his walls are bare. He has added no paintings. A single sketch hangs over his studio—Roark's original drawing of the Stoddard Temple. When they are seated side by side, he tells her what she desires to know without her asking. Roark is in Clayton, Ohio, constructing a new building for Janer's Department Store. He tells her it is five stories tall and located on Main Street; Roark has been there for about a month.

On her way to Reno, Dominique gets off the train in Clayton, Ohio. She arrives in the evening, and, after asking directions, walks to Main Street. She walks until she reaches the glare of an excavation site. The workers are working late. When Roark comes up to the street he sees Dominique. Noticing the expression on her face, he says, "You'd better sit down." He takes her suitcase and guides her to the steps of a vacant house across the street. She questions him about his room and the restaurants in which he eats. She asks him if people look at him as he sits at a lunch counter or walks down the street., and he tells her they do not. Because Dominique is still afraid of sharing him with lunch wagons and people on the street, Roark realizes that she has not come to stay. She says that the two country homes he's done in the past two years—one in Pennsylvania and the other near Boston—were "unimportant" buildings. "Inexpensive," he corrects her, but interesting to design. She says that what he has been working on is like the quarry all over again; that it is a major comedown—after the Enright House and the Cord Building—to build five-story structures for the rest of his life. Dominique tells Roark that she is going to Reno to obtain a divorce from Keating, and that she will then marry Gail Wynand. He thinks of Henry Cameron and his warning that the Wynand papers and everything they stand for is the symbol of their opposition. But Roark does not try to stop her. Suddenly, Dominique blurts out that she wants to live in this town with him; to have a small home that she will keep; that he will give up architecture; that they will live only for their love for each other, and nothing more. He answers that, were he cruel, he would accept, if only to see how long it would be before she begged him to return to architecture. When he walks her to the train station, he tells her their separation will last until she learns not to notice the contrast between him and the rest of society, until she learns not to be tormented by his struggle to succeed on his own terms. She boards the train and departs for Reno.

Dominique marries Wynand. Over the first months of their marriage she sees the best within him—his creative drive and his love of mankind's noblest accomplishments. Gradually, despite her contempt for his pandering, she comes to respect his virtues and to care for him. She warns him against Ellsworth Toohey's schemes to take over *The Banner*, but he merely laughs contemptuously. She tells him to go after Toohey and to destroy him. She points out that he doesn't understand Toohey, doesn't see that Toohey's real goal is to control the Wynand papers as a means of controlling the world. But Wynand knows that Toohey could not create *The Banner*, that he is incapable of such a feat, and he cannot conceive of Toohey as a threat to him or the world. He believes Dominique suffers from a "horror complex," and contemptuously dismisses the idea that Toohey could gain control of *The Banner*.

Commentary

The character of Gail Wynand is emphasized in this part. Wynand is a man of genius and consummate artistic judgment, who publishes yellow-press tabloids that do not reflect his own thinking or values, but rather those of the lowest tastes of the crowd. Wynand's pandering and self-betrayal are brought about by his quest for power.

Growing up on the tough streets of Hell's Kitchen, Wynand accepts the false law of this human "jungle"—that in life one either kills or is killed, rules or is ruled, eats or is eaten. Wynand chooses to rule. He believes that the men of competence and ability are rare flashes of talent in a world of mediocrity. The only means by which the few rational individuals can survive is by gaining power over the mindless dolts who, Wynand believes, form the overwhelming bulk of humanity. He, therefore, panders to the vulgar tastes of the crowd in order to gain wealth and influence.

Despite the way Wynand makes money off of giving the crowd what it wants, Wynand's better qualities are still alive. Like Dominique, he reveres the greatest achievements of mankind. Wynand so admires the skyline of New York City that he would fling his body into space, if possible, to protect the buildings in case of attack. He speaks knowingly of love as "total passion for the total height." His private art gallery contains only works of rare distinction. Because of Wynand's man-worship, his reverence for human beings at their most exalted, he not only loves Dominique but also, later, Roark's buildings and character.

Wynand and Dominique are—as Dominique points out—variations on a theme. They have committed the same error. Both believe that genius and integrity have no chance in this world, that only the most corrupt make it to the top, and that, therefore, one must choose between a debased success and a noble failure. The Henry Camerons and Howard Roarks of the world will be commercial failures. It is the Guy Francons and Peter Keatings who will be successful. In the face of such an alternative, Dominique and Wynand make different choices. Dominique will seek no value from such a world; she withdraws from it. She tries to give up her relationship with Roark and, though brilliant, pursues no independent career. She chooses to seek no values in a world where noble values are rejected. In order to maintain her spiritual purity, Dominique repudiates the world. She accepts noble failure.

But Wynand chooses the other alternative. "You don't run things around here, kid," was the standard response from fools to his youthful suggestions for innovations. Determined that he will, indeed, run things, he sells his soul for the wealth and power that his vulgar tabloids bring him. Wynand refuses to withdraw passively from a world of scoundrels. Rather, he becomes as ruthless as they are. A modern slang formulation of Wynand's view is that "either one swims with the sharks or one is eaten by them." Wynand chooses to swim with them—and, to a significant extent, swim as one of them. But the price he pays is enormous: his integrity.

Theme

Ayn Rand takes a stand on one of the most important questions of moral philosophy: What is the relationship between moral virtue and practical success? Between moral character and personal happiness? Do the two stand in inverse proportion to each other? The baseball manager, Leo Durocher, once said that "nice guys finish last"—the implication being that, in order to finish first, one must be not so nice a guy. Is this cynical view true? Is it the case that, if one lives an upright life committed to moral principles, then one has no chance of achieving worldly success? Many people—including influential philosophers—have believed, and continue to believe, that this is so. One must, therefore, make a choice—your soul or your wallet, your character or your practical success. Gail Wynand and Dominique Francon both accept this premise, although they make different choices.

But the story of *The Fountainhead* shows that Ayn Rand rejects this theory. Wynand lives in inner conflict, his commitment to the heroic in man undercut by his pandering and power-seeking. Eventually, when he attempts to use a corrupt instrument like *The Banner* to defend a genius like Roark, he is destroyed by the contradiction he has tried to live. Dedication to the noble cannot coexist in the same soul with pandering to the ignoble. Wynand's moral failings do not lead to success, but to its opposite: self-destruction.

Dominique comes to realize that her pessimism is mistaken. She sees that Keating not only fails in the end but does so because of his utter lack of moral backbone. She observes that Wynand not only moves toward some disaster but does so because he has sold his soul. She recognizes that, despite all of Toohey's scheming, he can neither stop Roark nor take control of *The Banner*; his evil is impotent against men who are morally superior. Most important, as the final part of the book illustrates, the unqualified success of Howard Roark shows Dominique that the good men not only *can* succeed in the world, but that they are the *only* ones who can. Good men alone can achieve success, because they keep their souls intact. Holding principles and values of one's own, and remaining true to them in action, is a necessary condition of success and happiness. Dominique sees all of this, and she changes her mind. It is not the sordid and corrupt who ultimately matter and triumph, she understands, but the clean and the incorruptible.

Theme

The life of Howard Roark—who achieves practical success not in spite of his high moral standards, but *because* of them—dramatizes Ayn Rand's theory that the moral and the practical are identical. This is an important sub-theme that runs throughout the book. The life of Peter Keating—his fall from the top, and the reasons for it—forms an important part of the lesson that Dominique learns. As his wife and, after the divorce, as an observer, Dominique watches carefully the events of Keating's life. Her marriage to him gives her a close-up view of both his methods and their results.

Dominique has been married to Keating for almost two years. Her attempt to "achieve" an anesthetized soul has failed. This is made clear by her visits to Mallory, her questions regarding Roark and his buildings, her stop to see Roark at the construction site in Ohio, her offer of marriage. Dominique is still in love with Roark, with the grandeur of his buildings and with the sight of human greatness. As Nietzsche remarked, "the noble soul has reverence for itself"—and such nobility of spirit is not to be lost. Ayn Rand quietly dramatizes an important moral point in this unsuccessful quest of Dominique's. Rand is in fundamental disagreement with the philosophy of Friedrich Nietzsche, because he subordinates reason to will or instinct in his understanding of how man gains knowledge. But Nietzsche does, at times, project an exalted view of the human potential, expressed in emotional, not intellectual terms. This is certainly true of the quote from Nietzsche's *Beyond Good and Evil* that Ayn Rand had at the head of her manuscript during the writing of *The Fountainhead*. Nietzsche says that there is "some fundamental certainty that a noble soul has about itself, something which is not to be sought, is not to be found, and perhaps also, is not to be lost."

Ayn Rand shows that Dominique, try though she might, cannot lose it. By some means early in her life—possibly through her exposure to great art—Dominique realized that the human potential contained far greater possibilities than the phony pretentiousness of her father and his ilk. Her reverence for the Greek statuette that she obtains in Part One shows her esteem for the Greek conception of man—for the exalted creed that man is capable of great things. Even though the men around her reject her noble vision, even though they prefer Wynand's *Banner* to Mozart or Michelangelo, Dominique knows that mankind is capable of great stature. This reverence for mankind's highest possibilities is the only religion that Dominique accepts. She is a committed hero-worshipper. When one has once glimpsed the sublime, it is exceedingly difficult, perhaps impossible, to ever again take seriously the profane. When one understands that an Aristotle, Leonardo, Newton, or Roark is possible—and more, when one yearns for such a sight of man's achievements—it is inconceivable that a Keating, much less a Toohey, could establish a beachhead in one's soul. Although Dominique believes that Roark will be destroyed, she knows that he is possible; such nobility of soul and greatness of achievement can be attained. Dominique values this truth the way Jeanne d'Arc values her faith. She, too, would burn at the stake rather than renounce it. To express this point by means of metaphor, Dominique aspires for a cathedral, where she can be uplifted in exalted consecration to the divine. She is unwilling to settle for a filth-ridden hovel as a substitute. Submersion in a cesspool would certainly dirty Dominique's body but would leave untouched the purity of her soul. Indeed, the very absence of sparkling cleanliness would serve only to underscore its importance to her. Immersion in the life of Keating, or of Wynand at his worst, cannot begin to alter Dominique's noble vision of human life. Nothing could.

Toohey recognizes that marriage to Keating has left Dominique untouched and unchanged. Because she is one of the few to recognize Toohey's true nature, she is a dangerous enemy. Toohey seeks to eradicate Dominique's hero worship and speculates that becoming Wynand's mistress may serve that purpose. Toohey hopes that life as Wynand's mistress—surrounded by the opulent splendor that is the fruit of Wynand's pandering—will make Dominique cynical; that she will renounce her commitment to integrity and heroism and surrender to the world's corruption in weary resignation. Toohey has a vested interest in the destruction, or at least the anesthetizing, of Dominique's devotion to the nobility of man. As long as she still loves man at his highest and best, she may choose to actively oppose Toohey's attempt to enslave mankind; she might decide to employ her intellect and talent as weapons in a battle against Toohey. This is a danger that Toohey fervently wishes to avoid. But important as this is, it is Toohey's minor reason for scheming to bring Dominique and Wynand together. His primary purpose is a desire to distract Wynand's attention from *The Banner*. As part of his ongoing campaign to eliminate any possibility of success for independent men, Toohey seeks to elevate a series of unthinking followers to positions of cultural eminence. His belief is that if society can be convinced that a fraudulent mediocrity like Keating or Gus Webb is a great architect, then society will be unable to comprehend or appreciate the work of a true genius like Roark. To this end, Toohey seeks to promote Lois Cook. If society accepts Cook as a great writer, then it becomes even more difficult for a Roark-like author to be recognized. Toohey has gotten his minions on *The Banner* to plug her book, *The Gallant Gallstone*, at every opportunity. Despite the subtlety of Toohey's orchestration, Wynand recognizes it and has this endorsement stopped. Wynand, as he puts it, does not allow people to amuse themselves on his paper. Toohey, who seeks to control editorial policy on the paper, is faced with a very smart and very tough adversary. Because Wynand is a notorious womanizer, and Dominique is not merely beautiful, but even more, shares his love of the exalted, Toohey hopes that involvement with Dominique will leave him so smitten that his attention to the details of his work will slacken. So Toohey brings Dominique into Wynand's life.

Toohey's scheme to divert Wynand's attention by introducing him to Dominique succeeds at one level, although at a deeper level it is an unmitigated disaster. Wynand's love for Dominique *does* keep him from paying full attention to *The Banner*. But Toohey knows that Wynand's *marriage* to Dominique means trouble. It is more than the specific danger represented by her knowledge and values. Dominique *does* warn Wynand regarding Toohey's true motives—and she *does* urge him to destroy Toohey before it is too late. But Wynand is too contemptuous of Toohey to heed the warning. The real danger lies in that she (and, later, Roark) causes in Wynand a heightened sense of his own values. "What's gotten into him?" wonders Alvah Scarrett, when Wynand kills pieces of trite conventionality. Toohey knows better. He fully realizes that Wynand's true soul is committed to the exalted in life, not the trite, sentimental, or vulgar. It's not a matter of what has gotten into Wynand, but of what is finally getting out. If *The Banner* becomes Wynand's paper, and not that of the people, then there is no room on it for the views of Ellsworth Toohey.

The relation of Toohey to Wynand is utterly parasitical. Wynand, for all his errors, is a creative power, a life force. He has risen out of the slums to create a vast empire by means of his own talent and effort. His newspapers and magazines, his real estate developments, are his creations. Toohey cannot match this. Toohey is incapable of creative work. What Toohey does is insinuate himself into Wynand's organization, then slither into a position of influence. Toohey cannot create *The Banner*; what he seeks to do is take it over.

In this way, Toohey's relation to Wynand parallels Keating's relation to Roark. Keating, incapable of original designs, needs Roark to create his buildings. Similarly, Toohey, incapable of any creative act, needs Wynand to provide him with a platform. When Wynand later pulls that platform away, Toohey is powerless. He needs to start over at a new paper, looking to worm his way into a position of power. Dependents like Keating and Toohey are helpless if the independent men they prey on refuse to carry them.

Roark's independence continues unabated. Despite the Stoddard scandal and the Depression, he continues to build. The jobs are small, inexpensive, and not well known; he builds nothing in New York City for five years—but he is working. Rare clients who like his work seek him out. The owner of the Ohio department store that he constructs saw his buildings in New York and liked them. This is the reason for all the commissions he receives. The Enright House and the Cord Building are major structures. Pictures of the Stoddard Temple remain in existence. The Heller house has stood by this time for years. Roark understands that all he needs is one prospective client to understand his buildings—to recognize their brilliant efficiency—and he will have a job. This is, gradually, what happens. Despite all that Toohey and an uncomprehending public can do, Howard Roark moves forward as an architect.

Glossary

pandering the sell-out of higher values to gain popularity and influence, such as by catering to the vulgar tastes of the crowd. Here, it applies to Gail Wynand and his newspaper.

self-betrayal to surrender the things most important to the self, generally in order to win approval from the group. Here, it applies to both Keating and Wynand, though in different forms.

Hell's Kitchen an area on the west side of Manhattan in New York City that in the late-nineteenth and early-twentieth centuries was a tough slum neighborhood. Here, it is the area in which Gail Wynand is born and raised.

cynicism a theory of human nature, holding that no virtue is possible to man, that all men are corrupt in some form. Here, it is the mistaken view that Wynand accepts from his tough upbringing.

Friedrich Nietzsche (1844–1900) German philosopher who held that certain superior men were beyond the traditional precepts of good and evil, and had the right to seek power over others. Here, it is the mistaken view held by Wynand that leads to his downfall.

Part Four
Howard Roark

Summary

In the spring of 1935, Howard Roark completes a summer resort, Monadnock Valley, in the mountains of Pennsylvania. Monadnock Valley is both an artistic and a commercial triumph. Customers love Roark's concept and design, and they flock to it. A young college graduate sees it as he rides his bicycle through wooded trails. Despite his youth, he is disillusioned by what he has been taught in college—that an individual owes selfless service to the community, that society comes first, and that virtue resides in sacrifice for one's fellow men. He finds a sense of exultation only amidst the beauties of nature. Among the works of men—surrounded by the pool halls and billboards—he experiences a sense of despair. He does not want to despise man or the works of man; he wants to admire them. But he finds little worthy of admiration. The young man had always wanted to write music, because the special sense of life that he finds so generally elusive has been captured by mankind's greatest composers. He thinks that men have not found the words for it, nor the deed, nor the thought, but they have found the music. He seeks to find the promise of that music made real in some act of man on earth. He's not looking for sacrifice or suffering or selflessness—but for joyousness. He does not ask his brothers or sisters to work for his happiness, but to show him theirs. He needs the sight of it, because he needs to know that it is possible. He wants to see human achievement made real. The knowledge of it will give him courage for his own. At the top of a hill, he sees the broad expanse of a valley below him. He sees houses of plain fieldstone—like the rocks jutting from the green hillsides—"and of glass, great sheets of glass used as if the sun were invited to complete the structures, sunlight becoming part of the masonry." He knows, by looking at the hillside, that someone understood how to build without altering the natural contours or beauty of the terrain. The houses were separate, cut off from each other, utterly distinct and individualized. The young man gapes. Then he notices that he is not alone. Some steps away from him, a man sits on a boulder and gazes at the valley below. He is absorbed in the sight. The man is tall and gaunt and has orange hair. The college graduate approaches the man respectfully and asks him if the sight before them is real. The man replies that is. It's not a movie set or a trick, the younger man wants to know. No, Roark, the orange-haired man tells him. It's a summer resort just completed that will be opened in a few weeks. "Who built it?" the boy wants to know. "'I did.' 'What's your name?' 'Howard Roark.' 'Thank you,' said the boy." The boy knows that the perceptive eyes looking at him understand everything that those words convey. Roark bows his head, in acknowledgment. The boy wheels his bicycle down the slope of the hill toward the houses in the valley, and Roark looks after him. "He had never seen that boy before and he would never see him again. He did not know that he had given someone the courage to face a lifetime."

Roark had not understood the reasons that he was hired to build Monadnock Valley. He had heard of it a year and a half before, in the fall of 1933. He had gone to see Caleb Bradley, who headed the company building the resort, and who was doing a good deal of promotion. Bradley's face reveals no flicker of emotion as Roark describes his plan, but he asks one strange question. Bradley asks if Roark was the architect who designed the Stoddard Temple. When Roark answers that he was, Bradley states it was funny he hadn't thought of Roark himself. Several days later, Bradley calls and asks Roark to explain his idea to Bradley's partners. Roark presents his plan: the worst curse of poverty, he says, is the lack of privacy. The rich can enjoy their summer vacations because they have their private estates to which they can retire. But people of good taste and small income have no place to go to escape the crowded conditions of the city. As Roark explains how to build cheaply not one huge hotel but many small, private ones, the men exchange occasional glances. Roark feels certain that they are the type of glances people exchange when they cannot laugh at the speaker aloud. But it could not have been that, he thought, because several days later he signs a contract to build the Monadnock Valley Resort.

Roark remembers his experience building the Stoddard Temple, and he demands Bradley's initials on every drawing that comes out of his drafting rooms. Bradley is eager to initial, sign, and approve. Beyond keeping a close watch over the budget, he is not involved himself in the project and leaves Roark in complete control. Roark is able to discover little about Bradley, and then loses interest in him altogether. He is building his greatest assignment. For a year, he lives at the construction site. Steven Mallory does the fountains and all the sculptural work for the resort, and he comes to live at the site long before he is needed. Roark's old draftsmen come to work for him again, some leaving better jobs in the city. When Mike Donnigan arrives with the crew of electricians, Mallory observes that the look on Mike's face matches Mallory's feeling that this project is more than a building, it is a crusade. Slowly, over the course of a year, the buildings of the resort are completed. But occasionally, Mr. Bradley visits the construction site, smiles blandly and departs, leaving Mallory with an unexplained anger—and fear.

Several months after the resort's completion, in the fall of the year, Roark and Mallory discover the reason for that fear. The resort is commercially successful. Roark had been correct in his conviction that there was a need for this kind of vacation spot. Even though Mr. Bradley's staff virtually stopped advertising the place, within a month of its opening every house in Monadnock Valley was rented. The vacationers love the design, and word of mouth causes the resort to become private news. One magazine, unsolicited, prints four pages of photographs of Monadnock Valley and sends a writer to interview Roark. Before the end of the season, the houses are leased in advance for the following year. In October, the story hits the newspapers that Mr. Bradley and his gang built Monadnock Valley as a swindle. They acquired the land for very little and sold two hundred percent of its stock. They thought it was too out of the way and inaccessible, not near any train or bus lines. They thought the time was not right, that the low income of the Depression era precluded the construction of a successful resort. They had an ingenious scheme for declaring bankruptcy when the place failed, as they were sure it would. They chose Roark as the worst crank they could unearth to design the place, and thought that his plan for individualized recreational areas was an antisocial idea. They prepared for every contingency except success. Therefore, they cannot go on, because now they have to pay back twice the amount the place earns in a year, and, as Mallory points out, it earns plenty. Bradley and his gang are arrested and face trial and possible prison time for their fraudulent scheme. But Roark understands that, although the owners will now sue each other, the place will not be torn down and neither he nor Mallory will be dragged into the legal wrangles. Quietly, he goes on with his work.

Before Roark can rent a house at Monadnock Valley and spend the summer, as he intends, he is summoned back to New York to finally complete the construction of the Aquitania Hotel. He receives a telegram from Kent Lansing saying, "I told you I would, didn't I? It took five years to get rid of my friends and brothers, but the Aquitania is now mine—and yours. Come to finish it." After five years of legal battles, Kent Lansing now owns it outright; Lansing and Roark finish it together. Roark sees the rubble and the dust cleared away from the building's girders. He sees the unfinished symphony completed and its light glowing at night in the city's skyline.

Roark has been busy in the last two years. The resort at Monadnock Valley was not his sole job. From different parts of the country, requests came for him. The reasons were always the same: Individuals were in New York and liked the Enright House, the Cord Building, or both; or someone saw a picture of the Stoddard Temple and loved it. He designed these new structures—shops, private homes, small office buildings—on trains and planes that carried him from the construction site at Monadnock Valley to these far-off towns: "It was as if an underground stream flowed through the country and broke out in sudden springs that shot to the surface at random, in unpredictable places." These are small jobs that do not generate publicity, but Roark is designing and building as he wants.

Because the financing behind the construction of Monadnock Valley is revealed to be fraudulent, there is a scandal in art circles as well as a trial, but Roark is not directly involved. Austen Heller writes an impassioned article in defense of Roark's genius that creates a stir among those interested in the arts. Heller describes the buildings Roark has designed and the brilliant innovativeness of his work. He exhorts his readers to understand and appreciate the achievements of Roark's career—and he does so not in his usual calm tones, but as an outraged cry against injustice: "And may we be damned if greatness must reach us through fraud!"

Ellsworth Toohey is worried. The commercial success of Monadnock Valley, the completion of the Aquitania Hotel, and the publicity generated by Heller's article have once again brought Roark to the forefront of public attention. Toohey breaks his general silence regarding Roark to attack the architectural qualities of the Monadnock resort. He writes that Caleb Bradley's morals were certainly questionable, but his artistic judgment was impeccable. Bradley, Toohey claims, was martyred by the bad taste of his customers. "In the opinion of this column his sentence should have been commuted in recognition of his artistic discrimination. Monadnock Valley is a fraud—but not merely a financial one." Roark's fame causes little change among the established gentlemen of great wealth, who are responsible for the preponderance of architectural commissions. Where previously their response was "Roark—never heard of him," now it is, "Roark—he's too sensational." But there are entrepreneurs who are impressed by the simple fact that Roark made money at Monadnock for owners who did not want to make money. "This was more convincing than abstract artistic discussion." Roark is gaining recognition. In the year after Monadnock, he builds two private homes in Connecticut, a movie theater in Chicago, and a hotel in Philadelphia. In the fall of 1936 Roark moves his office to the top floor of the Cord Building. At the time he designed it, he had intended that one day he would have his office there. He stops and looks briefly at the sign on the door that says simply, "Howard Roark, Architect." His inner office contains three walls of glass, high over the city, from which he can see the Enright House, the Aquitania Hotel, and far to the south, the Dana Building designed by Henry Cameron. On a rainy day in November, returning from a construction site on Long Island, he is accosted by his secretary, who tells him that he just received an important phone call. He has an interview the following afternoon with Gail Wynand.

As Roark enters the building housing *The New York Banner*, he reflects that Gail Wynand is the man whom he has come nearest to hating in his life. Wynand is both the symbol of the mindless conventionality that Henry Cameron saw as his primary enemy—and the husband of Dominique. Roark enters Wynand's office prepared to refuse any commission he is offered. Wynand, in turn, believes this interview will go exactly as all previous interviews with architects have gone: He merely has to speak to convey what he wants. The architect then nods in understanding, and the interview ends. But when Roark and Wynand meet face to face, neither of them is certain that there is not a moment when each stops in his normal course of movement. There is a moment when each forgets the immediate reality—when Wynand forgets the building he wishes to construct, and Roark is oblivious to the fact that this man is Dominique's husband—and focuses solely on the man he meets. There is one instant in which there is "only the total awareness, for each, of the man before him, only two thoughts meeting in the middle of the room—'This is Gail Wynand'—'This is Howard Roark.'"

Wynand intends to build a private home in Connecticut, and has purchased five hundred acres for that purpose. He has taken a long time to choose his architect. He has traveled around the country looking at buildings—at homes, at hotels, at office buildings. He never before heard of Roark. But then he saw Monadnock Valley, and recognized it as a masterpiece. After that, whenever he sees a building he likes, he asks who the architect is, and he always receives the same answer: Howard Roark. Wynand states that he wishes his home to have "the Roark quality," a sense of a joy that is so demanding and uplifting that it "makes one feel as if it were an achievement to experience it." Roark accepts the commission and Wynand explains his thinking regarding the home he wants.

Wynand desires a fortress in the country, so that he will not have to share Dominique with the people of the city. He tells Roark that he feels something much worse and much stronger than jealousy, that he cannot stand to see her on the streets of the city and must take her away from any contact with the shops, the streets, the taxicabs. He wants a fortress in which Dominique will be touched by neither the conventional lives of the men of the city nor the vulgar affairs of *The Banner*. He wants his home to be a vault to guard treasures too precious for the sight of men, but more, a world so beautiful that Dominique will not miss the one she's left. Wynand wants something sacred. He asks Roark if he's ever built a temple. He wants a temple built to Dominique Wynand—and he hires Roark to build it. He chooses Roark—even though he was away at the time of the Stoddard Temple and knows nothing about it—because what he sees in the Monadnock Valley Resort and in Roark's other buildings conveys a quality of the sublime akin to religion. He tells Roark that, when he finds an artist whose work he admires, he refuses to meet him, out of fear that the creator will not match his creation. When he meets Roark, however, Wynand realizes that this is one case in which an artist matches the greatness of his work. When Roark departs, Wynand has the paper's morgue send him all the material it has on Howard Roark and his career.

Alvah Scarrett hears of Roark's visit to Wynand's office, and tells Toohey. Both are concerned regarding the change that Dominique has wrought in their boss's attitude—by how he now kills popular pieces of trite sentimentality that he formerly published. But Toohey has succeeded in the past several years in placing his followers in positions of influence on *The Banner*. He tells Scarrett that if it comes to a showdown regarding control of the paper, the two of them do not have to worry about Gail Wynand any longer. Toohey is confident that he now has the power to control the newspaper.

Wynand and Roark become close friends, drawn together by their mutual love of man's highest accomplishments. Wynand makes clear how much he admires Roark's rise from humble origins. Nevertheless, driven by an uncontrollable lust to prove to himself that there are no men of integrity, he attempts to bribe and intimidate Roark into selling his soul for profit. He offers to build the home exactly as Roark has designed it, and to hire Roark as the exclusive architect for all future Wynand construction projects. In exchange for such a massive boost to his career, Wynand demands that all future Roark buildings be designed in compliance with traditional standards. He wants Roark to "build Colonial houses, Rococo hotels and semi-Grecian office buildings." He warns Roark that, should he refuse, Wynand will use his considerable influence to make sure that no future commissions will be offered to him, and that even the work gangs and granite quarries will be closed to him. Roark knows that Wynand is serious. He responds by telling Wynand that what the newspaperman wants is easy. He reaches for a slip of paper on Wynand's desk and proceeds to draw an adaptation of Wynand's home—but "with Colonial porches, a gambrel roof, two massive chimneys, a few little pilasters, a few porthole windows." He shows Wynand the sketch and asks if this is what he wants. Wynand gasps involuntarily. "Good God, no!" "Then shut up," said Roark, "and don't ever let me hear any architectural suggestions." Wynand slumps in his chair, defeated, and asks Roark if he realizes what kind of a chance he has taken. Roark says he took no chance, that he had an ally he could trust. When Wynand asks, "What, your integrity?" Roark replies, "Yours, Gail." Wynand realizes that he has finally met a man whose spirit cannot be broken. The results in Wynand's life, in the long run, will be monumental.

Wynand shows Roark's sketch of their home to Dominique, who knows the designer without seeing the signature or asking his name. When he tells her that Roark is coming that night to dinner, Dominique is stunned but manages not to show it. At the meal, Dominique is angered by Wynand's close familiarity with Roark and by Roark's obvious respect and affection for her husband. She mentions the Stoddard Temple, to remind Wynand that he has no right to Roark's friendship, but when Wynand responds with the appropriate guilt Roark tells him sincerely to forget that incident. Dominique, in love with Roark but married to Wynand, is tortured by their growing closeness. When Wynand visits Roark's office and goes to dinner with him alone, Dominique must acknowledge that, under the present circumstances, she has no right to visit Roark but Gail Wynand does.

Wynand summons Toohey into his office and informs him that he is forbidden to write one word about Roark in *The Banner*. Toohey smiles easily and replies that, at present, he has no need to write about Howard Roark.

Peter Keating's career is slipping. Toohey pushes Gus Webb, and Keating has been replaced by a newer fad. In desperation, Keating comes to Toohey, the power behind a new government housing project, Cortlandt Homes. Toohey gives Keating the specifications, but Keating knows he can't do it. He asks Roark to design it for him and to allow him to put his name on it. Roark agrees on one condition: that it be erected exactly as he designs it.

Roark designs Cortlandt; his plan solves the structural problems and is accepted. As construction begins, he and Wynand depart for a long cruise on his boat, the *I Do*. When they return, Roark finds that his plans have been altered. Although Keating has tried to protect the integrity of Roark's design, he has found it impossible against the bureaucratic power wielded by Toohey. Gus Webb and Gordon L. Prescott, two proteges of Toohey, have connections among the government officials in charge of the project, and get themselves appointed as associate designers. The changes in Roark's design begin with one of the social workers assigned to the Cortlandt development. She demands an added wing for a gymnasium, although there are two schools and a Y.M.C.A. within walking distance. Webb and Prescott both desire to express their individuality, and Toohey sees no reason to hold them back. Keating trudges from office to bureaucratic office, seeking to preserve Roark's building, but finds no one willing to assume responsibility for "an issue of esthetics." Roark, after seeing an announcement in the newspaper describing Webb and Prescott as associates, stands across the future road from the construction site and stares at what had once been his design. "He saw the economy of plan preserved, but the expense of incomprehensible features added . . . a new wing added, with a vaulted roof, bulging out of the wall like a tumor. . . ." The evening after Roark's return, Keating comes uninvited to Roark's apartment. Sincerely contrite regarding his inability to prevent the alterations to Roark's building, Keating offers to openly confess the truth in public, but Roark declines. He does not tell Keating his plan, but points out that the consequences of his impending action will be worse for him than for Keating.

With Dominique's assistance, Roark dynamites the building. Although he does not need her help, he judges that she is now rid of the belief that the good has no chance at success, and is consequently free to take an active role in aiding him. She pretends to run out of gas in front of Cortlandt, and sends the night watchman to get gas at the nearest service station, one mile away. With no lives endangered, Roark then blows up the building. He turns himself in and says he will speak at the trial.

There is public outrage against the destruction of a housing project. For the first time in his career, Wynand goes against public opinion. He defends Roark in *The Banner*. Wynand maintains that his newspaper controls public opinion, and that his readers will believe what he wants them to believe. He personally takes charge of the campaign to defend Roark, putting on display his own brilliant journalistic skills in the process. He writes a series of articles describing trials in which innocent men were unjustly convicted by the ignorant bias of society. *The Banner* recounts the history of those great thinkers persecuted by an uncomprehending public—Socrates, Galileo, Pasteur, and many others. Wynand runs an exposé of the public housing industry: "the graft, the incompetence, the structures erected at five times the cost a private builder would have needed." He puts out the word to his twenty-two newspapers, his magazines, and his newsreels: Defend Roark, demonstrate his innocence, reshape public opinion. But because Roark blew up a housing project for the poor, opinion runs heavily against him. The backlash against his defenders is swift and strong. There is an outcry against Wynand, and circulation drops. The strongest elements of dissent come from Wynand's own public—from the Women's Clubs, the ministers, the mothers, the small shopkeepers. "Roark was almost forgotten in the storm of indignation against Gail Wynand." For several years, the popularity of *The Banner* had been dropping, as Wynand, inspired by Dominique's presence to display his real values, had killed many of the sentimental pieces adored by his public. Further, Toohey had subtly orchestrated a campaign against Wynand featured in the small but prestigious intellectual magazines. Now, stickers and posters proclaiming, "We Don't Read Wynand," appear on walls and subways across New York City. Many news vendors refuse to display *The Banner*; they carry it hidden under their counters, to be provided for customers only on request: "The ground had been prepared, the pillars eaten through long ago; the Cortlandt case provided the final impact."

Toohey now judges the moment propitious to strike. When Wynand is out of town, he goes against policy and attacks Roark in *The Banner*; Wynand fires Toohey. The union of Wynand employees, organized and controlled by Toohey, goes out on strike. Wynand and Dominique, with virtually no assistance, put out the paper by themselves; it comes back unread. The newspaper's board of directors meets and points out the huge sums of money *The Banner* is losing. Mitchell Layton, a wealthy follower of Toohey, who owns the second largest block of the paper's stock, offers to buy Wynand out. The board makes clear that the choice is simple: Either accept back the men fired and alter the paper's stand on Roark, or close the newspaper. Wynand relents; in order to save *The Banner* he agrees to publicly reverse his position on the Cortlandt dynamiting.

Dominique leaves him and moves in with Roark, who awaits trial. On their first morning together, she calls the police and newspapers to report her jewelry stolen in the night. She knows that the story of

Mrs. Wynand spending the night alone with another man—especially the accused dynamiter, Howard Roark—will be front page news on the New York tabloids. Dominique realizes that if Gail Wynand, in order to save the tawdry, pandering *Banner*, publicly calls the noble Roark "a reprehensible character, a dangerous, unprincipled, antisocial type of man," then justice requires his own wife and reputation to be offered up to his public in as lurid a story as possible. Even though Dominique knows that what she is doing makes it harder for Roark, that it adds scandal to everything else society throws at him, she is happy. For now she is unafraid of society's judgment—willing to face whatever it does to her or to Roark—and is free to pursue her values.

At his trial, Roark defends the right of a creator to his creation. He argues that, through the centuries, individuals have had new ideas and developed new methods and processes, and often these individuals have been rejected by their peers because their theories or products were new and upset the established routine of people's lives. Roark points out that the first-handed creators have carried mankind on their backs, but have often been kicked in the teeth for their efforts. Roark had the new ideas that enabled Cortlandt to be built; the housing project was a product of his thinking, and remains his intellectual property. An individual is morally and legally entitled to be paid for his work, and the payment he demands is that the building be erected as he designed it. According to this definition, Roark was not paid. Society gladly took the product of his mind and effort, but refused to pay him his asking price. This is an injustice. Because it is not possible to sue the government, he was left with no recourse but to blow up the project and make it a test case for the courts to decide. Roark stands for an individual's right to his own mind and to ownership of the product of his efforts. The jury understands Roark's argument, and he is acquitted. Roger Enright buys Cortlandt from the government and hires Roark to build it. Gail Wynand, though morally and psychologically broken, hires Roark to build the Wynand Building, the world's tallest skyscraper. Roark and Dominique marry. He has achieved both commercial and romantic success—and has done so on his own terms.

Peter Keating is exposed publicly as a fraud at the Cortlandt trial—and his career is finished. Ellsworth Toohey is reinstated to his position at *The Banner* by the labor board. Wynand has Toohey report back to work at 9:00 p.m. and waits for him in the door of his office. Wynand stands silently as Toohey arrives early and takes again his accustomed place at his desk. Toohey is made nervous by the specter of Wynand hanging over him in the doorway, but is reassured by the sound of the rolling presses—the constant accompaniment of a newspaperman's life. Then the presses stop. Wynand looks at his wristwatch and says, "It's nine o'clock. You're out of a job, Mr. Toohey. *The Banner* has ceased to exist." Wynand refuses to turn his life's work over to Toohey, so he closes the paper. Standing alone with the man he recognizes as the most contemptibly evil member of society, Wynand says, "This was the end of *The Banner* . . . I think it's proper that I should meet it with you." Toohey must start over again at another newspaper, having failed in his attempts to both stop Roark and to control Wynand's *Banner*.

Commentary

Part Four is dedicated to the triumph of Howard Roark. By the end of the story, Roark is in his late thirties and has endured significant hardships but now has everything he wants. His trial shows that his was the genius responsible for Cortlandt; his acquittal demonstrates recognition of his moral principles; his hiring by Enright and Wynand to build Cortlandt and the Wynand Building gives him both commercial success and fame; his marriage gives him an enduring intimate relationship with the woman he loves. How—by what means—was he able to triumph over such concerted social opposition?

The answer to this question goes to the heart of the book's meaning—to the role played by values in a man's life. A person's values are those things or persons he considers valuable, of significant worth; the things that fill his life with meaning and purpose. Roark's values are clear: He loves architecture of a certain kind—"my work done my way"—above all else. He loves his future wife, Dominique, and his dearest friend, Gail Wynand. These are of paramount importance in his life; other things are of lesser or of no value to him. One key point is that these are *his* values, chosen by Roark's own judgment. Unlike Keating, Roark does not go into architecture because his mother chooses it; nor does he marry Dominique because she impresses other people. Roark becomes an architect because the field fascinates him; he marries Dominique because he loves her. In Ayn Rand's revolutionary way of looking at moral issues, Howard Roark is profoundly *selfish*. He is a prime representative of what she calls "the virtue of selfishness."

The question regarding the sense in which selfishness is a virtue is raised at the end of Part One. Roark desperately needs the commission for the Manhattan Bank Building. Mr. Weidler fights for him, but the board keeps him waiting. Finally, they give it to Roark, but on one condition—they will alter his design. Roark refuses. The board members are incredulous; Roark is on the brink of utter destitution, yet he turns down a major commission in the heart of New York City in order to protect the integrity of his design. "Do you have to be quite so fanatical and selfless about it?" they ask. "That was the most selfish thing you've ever seen a man do," Roark responds, squeezing his drawings to his side.

Style & Language

The questions of how Roark's behavior is selfish—and of what is *virtuous* about selfishness—can be answered only in the context of the entire story. Ayn Rand challenges 2,500 years of moral philosophy in this book. "What does it mean to be selfish?" she asks. It can only mean, in its denotation, to be concerned with oneself—with one's *self*. But one's self consists of two components: the values that one chooses and the thinking or judgment that one uses to do the choosing. This issue of selfishness is the one that Roark's life dramatizes. Roark is true, under all circumstances, to his mind, to his judgment, to his values. He certainly wants the commission for the Manhattan Bank Building, and he wants the money and the career boost it will bring. But these are not as important to him as the integrity of his design. If he permits the adulteration of his design to gain the commission, it would constitute a *self-sacrifice*. It would involve giving up that which is more important to him for that which is less. Such a self-betrayal Roark refuses to make.

Roark realizes that his happiness requires his buildings to be erected as he designs them. Were he to compromise his design for fame and fortune, he would not be happy. Every time Roark looked at the building on which he had compromised—whenever he thought of it—he would experience only shame. Roark understands that happiness requires commitment, *in action*, to one's values. To surrender the things most important to him is a sacrifice that Roark will not make. His rejection of the Manhattan Bank commission is the act of remaining true to his values, that is, to his self—in action and under extreme duress. This scene in *The Fountainhead* often recalls Polonius' famous line to Laertes in Shakespeare's *Hamlet*—"To thine own self be true, and it follows as the night the day that thou cannot play false with any man." Polonius says it in *Hamlet*; Howard Roark lives it and shows what it looks like in *The Fountainhead*.

Character Insight

The board members of the Manhattan Bank Building accuse Roark of selflessness. This accusation is false. But there *is* a character in the story who is specifically designed by the author to be the essence of selflessness: Peter Keating. According to conventional ethics, Keating is a ruthless example of egotism. He lies, cheats, flatters, manipulates, and virtually murders Lucius Heyer in order to attain partnership in the country's most prestigious firm. It looks as though Keating does all this for himself. But Ayn Rand challenges us to analyze the issue at a deeper level. A self, she argues, is exactly what Peter Keating lacks.

If a person's self is the values he chooses and the independent judgment by means of which he makes the choices, then these are the very things Keating has abdicated. His values and his mind have been turned over to others. In his youth, for example, painting was a budding passion for him. Had Keating pursued painting, it may have brought him a fulfilling career. But he does not; he surrenders his desires in order to please his mother. Mrs. Keating is concerned with respectability; she wants social acceptance. To her, painting is a bohemian—not a respectable—lifestyle. An artist, after all, wears torn, paint-splattered jeans, he freezes in a garret in New York City's Soho district, he has nude women in his apartment as models. But architecture, she believes, offers a very different kind of life. Architects wear double-breasted, pin-striped, Brooks Brothers suits; they have offices on Park Avenue; they draw their clients from the Social Register. For these reasons, architecture is a respectable career. Keating gives up a career he would have loved not because he loves architecture more (he doesn't love it at all) but because others want him to. He surrenders a career in art not merely to meet his mother's expectations, but to meet her understanding of society's expectations. Keating is a conformist. Other people, not his own judgment, dominate his career choice. He is *selfless*.

A person generally pursues long-term happiness in two areas: career and love. Because Keating is not excited by architecture, he has condemned himself to a career of unrelieved drudgery. His one chance at lasting happiness lies in the area of romantic love. The good news is that he and Catherine Halsey love each other. The sincerity of Keating's love is shown by his refusal to use Katie. He desires to meet Ellsworth Toohey, the rising star of architectural criticism, whose patronage is sufficient to make or break an architect. Catherine, Toohey's innocent niece, is willing to introduce Keating to Toohey immediately, but Keating refuses. He confesses to her that he uses people, and vows that he will not do it to her; he wants their relationship clean, untainted by his manipulative methods. Gail Wynand says in another context that "love is the exception-making," that a person will do for the loved one things he would do for no other. Keating manipulates everyone. Katie is the only one he relates to honestly; she is the one exception in his life. He loves her and he would be happy with her. But he leaves her the night before his wedding to marry Dominique Francon.

Keating does not love Dominique; he does not even like her. Because Dominique sees clearly Keating's fraudulent nature and is unafraid to state the truth openly, she intimidates him. He jilts the woman he loves and marries a woman he does not love for the very reason he originally became an architect: to impress other people. Keating doesn't leave Katie just because she's plain. In addition to beauty, Katie lacks poise and elegance; she has none of the social graces that Dominique has. If Keating walks into the grand ballroom of the Waldorf-Astoria with Katie on his arm, not one head in the room will turn; no one will be impressed. But Dominique is quite another matter. In addition to her beauty, Dominique possesses the charm and poise lacking in Katie. She impresses people. This is the exchange Keating makes: He gives up the woman he loves and a lifetime of happiness in order to impress other people with the "trophy" wife he has in Dominique. Love and happiness for prestige—this is the trade Keating makes. Again, Keating betrays what he wants, and what will make him happy, in order to gain social approval.

The deeper point in Keating's life is that, in giving up his values, Keating gives up his mind. His life is no longer ruled by what he thinks, knows, and wants—but by what others believe and want. Their values and thinking now govern his life, not his own. Keating has abdicated his self; he has betrayed it so fully that, by the end of the story—before he is even forty—there is nothing left of him. He is an empty shell of a man, with nothing uniquely his own. Every personal vestige has been sacrificed in order to please others. He has reached a state of selflessness in its literal meaning—he is without self. He is the opposite of Howard Roark.

The results of selfishness and selflessness are obvious. Roark, no matter the duration and difficulty of his struggle, is on a *value*-quest; his life is filled, from top to bottom, with the things he loves. A life full of designing structures like the Aquitania Hotel and the Enright House, of intimate moments with the woman he loves, of hours with friends such as Wynand, Mallory, Mike Donnigan, and, of course, Henry

Cameron—this is the impassioned, value-driven existence of Howard Roark. Even though at times he struggles, Roark has surrounded himself from morning until night with the things, people, and activities most important to him. Roark's life, therefore, is an ongoing love affair.

The exact opposite is true of Keating. He has abandoned the things most important to him—painting and a relationship with Catherine Halsey. The things his day is filled with—architecture and a relationship with Dominique Francon—are not important to him. His life is a series of meaningless actions, an existence of drudgery. For several years, he has all the prestige and social approval a man can ask for, but this is external. Internally, he has nothing. The heartbreaking scene near the end, when Keating returns to his abandoned childhood love—painting—and brings his canvases to Roark, shows this. Roark, looking at the crude, childish work, is overcome with pity and can barely bring himself to speak the truth. But it is too late for Keating. A lifetime of betraying *his* mind, *his* thinking, *his* artistic judgment, has killed whatever creative spark he may have possessed long ago. Creativity, by its very nature is a *self*-driven activity; it is not borrowed from others. On the contrary, it necessarily involves new ideas, thoughts that others have not had. One can choose to follow the crowd or one can choose to be creative, but one cannot be both. Keating's stated lifelong policy, "Always be what people want you to be," is the credo of blind followers. As such, it is anathema to creativity. Consistent acts of self-betrayal cannot be performed with impunity.

Just as Roark's success relative to Keating's failure shows the virtue of selfishness and the evils of selflessness—so Roark's triumph over Toohey's machinations demonstrates another moral truth. Toohey is a highly intelligent, possibly brilliant individual, who, though lacking the creative abilities of Roark and Wynand, could have been an outstanding scholar had he made other choices. But for all the ingenious cunning of his schemes, Toohey fails utterly in his attempts to stop Roark and to take control of Wynand's newspaper. The reasons for Toohey's defeat go to the heart of Ayn Rand's philosophy. Every activity of Toohey's life is oriented toward other people. He critiques the work of others by reference to moral and aesthetic theories developed by still others in order to control and enslave others still. Not a single act of Toohey's life is creative. In other words, nothing he does is directed toward building or constructing something. He does not even hammer nails into wood to make a chair or paint the walls of his living room. Such creative activities as carpentry and house-painting are utterly alien to him. Toohey is helpless to deal directly with nature, with physical reality; his distinctive orientation is social. He seeks no mastery over nature but exclusively over men.

It is the very parasitism of Toohey's functioning that makes him dangerous. It is also what leaves him helpless. If he cannot perform constructive tasks, how is he to survive in a physical world? Only by insinuating himself into the souls of others and controlling them can he survive. Roark states in his courtroom address that the creator seeks to conquer nature and the parasite to conquer men. Toohey's helplessness in the face of reality drives him toward spiritual and social conquest. He must hold dominion over others in order to ensure his own survival. The larger Toohey's cult following, the more powerful the buffer between him and the physical world of which he is terrified. Victims like Keating and Catherine Halsey are not weaker—like antelopes devoured by a lion—but essentially *stronger* in their capacity to deal efficaciously with physical reality. Toohey must control them, for their very ability to perform at least some types of productive work is the lifeline he craves. Keating and Catherine are his sole source of survival, and so, like a vampire of the spirit, he sucks their lifeblood.

But Toohey is even worse than this. His power-seeking is not fundamentally motivated by a quest for survival, but by something significantly more evil. He doesn't merely fear the men capable of independent existence; he hates and desires to destroy them. In his childhood, he knew Johnny Stokes, "a bright kid with dimples and curls," whom people always turned to see. Because no one ever turned to look at Ellsworth Toohey, he turns the hose on Johnny. Years later, part of his scheming to involve Dominique first with Keating, then with Wynand, is a plainly stated intention to destroy this brilliant and beautiful woman. He openly seeks to ruin Roark's career and, in a confession speech at the end of the novel, Toohey answers Keating's question regarding a desire to kill Roark by stating that he wants Roark alive—but utterly broken. The question of the fate to befall the independent men of the world if and when Toohey reaches his goal of intellectual advisor to a Fascist or Communist dictator is clear: Just as he intends to imprison and break Roark, so he intends the same for Roark's comrades-in-spirit. Only two kinds of power exist in life: the power to create and the power to destroy. Toohey neither seeks nor attains the power to create. He possesses only the power to destroy—and he is particularly concerned with using it against the able and successful individuals whom he envies.

Toohey is a spiritual killer looking for an opportunity to become a physical one. He has the power to destroy. This power is limited, however, to conformists like Keating, who are looking for a master to follow—and to a panderer like Wynand, who allows Toohey a foothold in his organization because of the columnist's popularity. But over an independent man like Roark, who has no need of him—who does not even think of him—Toohey has no power. His power is limited to those victims who voluntarily grant him their souls or, at least, a beachhead in their lives. Those who grant Toohey nothing, like Roark and Dominique, are in no danger from him.

That Toohey's destructive capacity is limited is true—but it is a relatively minor point. The major point is that Toohey has no power to create. Ayn Rand's claim is that evil is irrational; it does not focus on reality, seeking to build, create, or grow; it focuses only on other men, seeking to enslave, control, and destroy. She calls this point the impotence of evil. Evil men are capable only of destruction, never of construction. They can tear down; they cannot build up. Toohey succeeds in destroying *The New York Banner*, but is incapable of recreating it after Wynand closes it. Any "victory" won by evil men is empty. They are incapable of creativity and—despite the number of souls they conquer, innocent lives they destroy, or dollars they loot—their lives are miserable. As Toohey tells Keating, "Enjoyment is not my destiny." Happiness comes from achieving values, from building and producing, not from desecrating and destroying.

Roark is a happy man. He creates value by bringing into the world new designs and structures. He is a builder and looks out at nature joyously: "He looked at the granite. To be cut, he thought, and made into walls. He looked at a tree. To be split and made into rafters." His life is filled exclusively with plans to build; even during the times with no clients, he studies the new materials and technologies, learning how to use them, working toward the day when he can apply this knowledge to build a Cortlandt Homes and other new buildings. Even working in a granite quarry is a means toward that end, for Roark saves money so that he can reopen his office and return to architecture. Roark, the independent thinker, is rational (focused on facts, on nature, on reality). This rationality is what enables him to build. Roark is an exemplar of the man who conquers nature, not other men. His rational functioning, like that of a scientist, is what enables him to achieve, build, and produce. Here is the positive side of the issue—the potency of the good. Only the good can achieve values. Only the good can deal effectively with reality. Only the good can create and build. In consequence, only the good can reach a state of flourishing life and experience joy.

Roark's triumph and Toohey's failure—the potency of the good and the impotence of the evil—explain another point in the story: the nature of Dominique's error. Dominique, for all her brilliance and idealism, is tormented by her pessimism—by her belief that the good and the noble have no chance in a corrupt world. While still young, Dominique sees her father wine and dine his way to the top of his profession, even though he is a mediocre architect. Dominique realizes that Henry Cameron is the world's greatest designer but sees that he is a commercial failure. In her twenties, Dominique finds Peter Keating on the fast track to success and Howard Roark consigned to a granite quarry. She observes that Ellsworth Toohey, the most evil creature imaginable, is hailed as a moral saint by millions of people. Her conclusion is that evil is a dominant force in man's life; that the good are weak and ultimately doomed. Ayn Rand terms such pessimism the *malevolent universe premise*. Its optimistic contrary, held by Roark, that the world is open to the achievement of values by the good, she calls the *benevolent universe premise*.

Dominique's view is mistaken, though given her experiences, understandable. The events of the story clearly dramatize Ayn Rand's benevolent universe theory. Dominique, an honest and acute observer, witnesses Roark's steady, if tortuous climb, Toohey's inability to reach either of his goals, Keating's decline and eventual exposure, Wynand's inability to succeed by the method of pandering—and she changes her mind. An early note of Dominique's transition is her warning to Wynand regarding Toohey. This warning signals more than a growing respect for Wynand's virtues; it indicates her shifting view regarding the world's moral nature. She no longer believes that the world deserves Toohey. She now sees that the world is better than that—and that it deserves better than the Fascist/Communist dictatorship Toohey seeks to impose. Her willingness to help Roark dynamite Cortlandt, though the action could well bring him imprisonment, shows her final liberation from the grip of her malevolent premise. Before the trial, Dominique says, "Howard . . . willingly, completely, and always . . . without reservations, without fear of anything they can do to you or me. . . . Howard, if you win the trial—even that won't matter too much. You've won long ago. . . ." Dominique understands that, regardless of social rejection, it is the independent thinkers like Roark who understand nature's laws, who make advances and who carry mankind forward. He is the creative man who gives life its meaning; he is the one who recognizes and lives up to man's highest potential. She now understands to whom the earth belongs—and it is to the creators, not the parasites; to the virtuous, not the guilty.

Roark's life, and its successful outcome, dramatizes the benevolent universe principle. The world is open to a *thinking* man's achievement of values. Conformists, nonconformists, and power-seekers cannot achieve values and be happy, because all of them, in one form or another, give up their minds to the crowd—the Keatings to follow, the Lois Cooks to spit defiance, the Tooheys to rule. Men who surrender their judgment have no chance at success or happiness. But the thinkers learn to grow food, to make fire, to build homes, to cure disease. They can flourish, and by means of their creative work, make flourishing life possible for the rest of mankind. The world is open to those independent thinkers who refuse to renounce their minds.

The novel's theme is expressed fully in the final section. The triumph of Roark, and the utter defeat of Keating and Toohey, represents the victory of the independent thinkers over the followers and parasites. Roark's courtroom speech explains the issues that lie at the heart of the book's meaning. He examines the contrast and conflict between those whom Ayn Rand terms *first-handers* and *second-handers*.

The *first-handers* are those who use their own minds. They do not accept ideas second-hand, merely because other people believe them. First-handers learn from others—like Roark learns from Cameron—but they do not copy or obey. Learning requires a thoughtful understanding, an autonomous recognition of an idea's truth; it is made possible only by a thinking process and is the opposite of the unthinking acceptance of the Keating-style conformist. All innovators, inventors, and discoverers of new knowledge are first-handers. Individuals like Edison, Pasteur, Copernicus, and Darwin—first-handers—are original thinkers, not glorified draftsmen copying the work of previous minds.

The *second-handers* are those who abdicate the responsibility of independent judgment. In one form or another, they allow the thinking of others to dominate their lives. They are unwilling to accept the arduous effort of thinking, and instead, exist as cognitive puppets of society, ruled by the ideas popular in their cultural milieu. They accept ideas second-hand—as hand-me-downs from others. All conformists, nonconformists, and power-seekers—the Keatings, Lois Cooks, and Tooheys—function in this manner. They are not thinkers, they are not focused on reality, they cannot and do not build. Their existence is entirely social; they accomplish nothing creative or innovative; they merely accept and copy.

The fundamental issue in life is survival. Roark spells out the life-and-death stakes in his courtroom speech. He points out that man comes onto earth with none of the goods necessary for his survival. Everything required for human life is a product of his own effort. According to Roark, man faces a constant alternative: He can survive by means of his own effort or as a leech fed by the productive work of others. "The creator originates. The parasite borrows. The creator faces nature alone. The parasite faces nature through an intermediary. The creator's concern is the conquest of nature. The parasite's concern is the conquest of men."

Jacob Bronowski, the American scientist and cultural historian, tells the story of the agricultural revolution, an example that bears out Roark's distinction. To the best of our knowledge, human beings first learned to grow crops and domesticate livestock in ancient Mesopotamia, in the fertile lands between the Tigris and Euphrates rivers. Prior to this, human societies had existed by means of hunting, a method dependent on weather conditions and limiting man to a sub-sistence level. But then some innovative thinkers figured out how to cultivate the soil—how to grow crops, fertilize the ground, irrigate dur-ing times of drought, and domesticate livestock. These farmers had a much higher standard of living than did the hunters living in the hills surrounding them. When drought struck, the farmers irrigated, but the hunters starved as the game migrated or died. The hunters then swept out of the hills with their spears and other weapons, murdered the peaceful farmers, stole the food, and gorged themselves. When the food ran out, they starved. Unable to grow the food, they too died.

The farmers are first-handers. They are Howard Roark-type inno-vators who deal directly with nature. By use of their own minds, they identify the means by which to create abundance. The hunters are sec-ond-handers. Unable or unwilling to perform the creative work neces-sary, they instead steal from those whose effort has produced the goods. They survive (briefly) as leeches. They are one type of parasite of whom Roark speaks.

Many other types of parasites exist. The Keating-style conformists can be found in many organizations and corporations, seeking to rise by manipulation, on the premise of "it's not what you know, it's who you know that counts." These individuals are "gravy train riders," per-forming no productive work themselves, but instead attempting to cash in on the work of others. Real life provides a multitude of second-handers, some barely touched upon in *The Fountainhead*. Family bums, welfare recipients, criminals, psychological manipulators, spiritual power seekers, political dictators, and military conquerors are all examples of those seeking a second-handed form of survival. All exist as leeches off the thoughts and work of more productive people.

Roark's courtroom speech is an impassioned defense of the first-handers—of their creative nature, their life-giving abilities, and their historical and present persecution. He speaks about the struggles of the great original thinkers—not merely of the effort spent to invent products or create new methods, but of the battles waged to get the new ideas a hearing. Roark points out that those battles were waged by the inventors against the very men who stood to benefit most from the innovations. "Throughout the centuries there were men who took first steps down new roads armed with nothing but their own vision. The great creators—the thinkers, the artists, the scientists, the inventors—stood alone against the men of their time. Every great new thought was opposed." But the creative thinkers, on fire with the truth of their visions, persevered; sometimes they were executed or otherwise silenced, but they refused to surrender, and, in the end, they triumphed. Though a myriad of second-handers may oppose and/or exist parasitically off of the creative thinkers, the first-handers are the great men who ultimately are responsible for human progress.

The distinction drawn between first- and second-handers is the answer to the question Roark poses in the book's opening pages. Roark wonders about "the principle behind the Dean." He understands men such as himself but is puzzled by those like the Dean. By the end of the novel, Roark is no longer puzzled. He understands that the key difference among human beings is not one of gender, race, nationality, or even intelligence—but of the method with which they use their minds. A man like the Dean, despite his intelligence and erudition, is a follower because his orientation is toward society; other people are the Dean's fundamental reality, so he necessarily seeks truth by looking to their beliefs. He is a good example of second-handedness, because his ideas, his standards, his values are borrowed from others. But Roark himself, he realizes, is oriented toward nature or physical reality; here, not in society, is where Roark looks in his search for truth. Roark embodies the essence of first-handedness, because his ideas, standards, and values are unborrowed; they are derived independently from reality.

Although the novel is not fundamentally about politics, the distinction between first- and second-handers has definite political-economic implications. These implications are made clear by examining several of the main characters in *The Fountainhead*. Toohey is the one character in the novel with political goals. He is a collectivist intellectual seeking to establish a Fascist/Communist dictatorship in America. Toohey knows that such a society is one of, for, and by the second-handers. Its appeal is its claim to provide cradle-to-grave care for an individual. A person will be born in a state-controlled hospital, raised in a state-controlled nursery, educated in a state-controlled school, employed in a state-controlled factory. In return for its generosity, the state requires only one thing of its citizens: obedience. Toohey realizes that there is no chance to form such a state with a citizenry of Howard Roarks. Such independent persons desire to support themselves; they will not be wards of the state—and they refuse to obey. But with a society of Peter Keatings, Toohey's goal is achievable. The Keatings will surrender their minds to a leader; they *want* to do so; they will obey in order to win approval from the rulers. Toohey, the aspiring power behind the throne of such a dictatorship, makes clear to Keating the world he envisions: "We'll enjoy unlimited submission—from men who've learned nothing except to submit. We'll call it 'to serve.' We'll give out medals for service. You'll fall over one another in a scramble to see who can submit better and more." Hence, Toohey's lifelong quest to induce submission in others.

Those individuals like Roark, who are psychologically independent, require political/economic independence. These individuals think for themselves and will not, under any circumstances, surrender their minds to a leader, whether religious, political, or other. They wish to live their own lives, pursue their own goals, seek their own happiness. Many have the entrepreneurial spirit and want to work for themselves. They will not exist as wards of the state, for they are not robotic automata. These individualists will create and thrive in a free country such as the United States. Just as the psychological dependence of a Keating leads to political/economic dependence, so the psychological independence of a Roark leads to political/economic independence. The conformists will voluntarily give up their minds and their freedom to a dictator like Hitler; the individualists will defend their freedom to the death.

In a free society, the Roarks of the world flourish. The freest country in history is the United States; and the height of its freedom was from the late nineteenth century (when the Emancipation Proclamation ended slavery in 1863) until the early twentieth century (when the socialist ideas of Marx began to win control of the American universities and political system). That era saw a plethora of inventions and new developments. The freedom of American society enabled the most independent minds—those real-life creators of whom Howard Roark is a fictitious representative—to think freely, to develop new ideas, to take those new products and methods to the marketplace, to convince the customers that the innovations were superior to the established ways of doing things, and to make a fortune. Independent thinkers like Roark require the freedom to act on their thinking. Without that, all of their thinking is fruitless. This is why the freest countries—the United States, Japan, Western Europe—are the most prosperous, and why dictatorships—whether of the Communist, military, or theocratic varieties—are significantly poorer. Given liberty, the Howard Roarks of society are free to innovate and create abundance; in the absence of liberty, the most independent minds are stifled, productivity is squashed, and the standard of living cannot rise. Independent minds are responsible for progress and prosperity; independent minds require freedom.

Glossary

egoism a moral theory urging an individual to attain his values and live a joyous existence. Here, it is lived by Roark in the form of *rational* egoism, the commitment to *earning* the things he wants by his own mind and effort.

altruism a moral theory urging an individual to sacrifice his values and happiness in order to serve others. Here, it is the code advocated by Ellsworth Toohey.

selfishness the commitment, in action, to one's self, i.e., one's own values; a persistent quest to achieve—and the refusal to betray—one's values for any reason. Here, it is embodied consistently in the life of Howard Roark.

selflessness the opposite of selfishness. A betrayal of the self by the surrender of one's values. Here, it is embodied in the life of Peter Keating.

first-hander an individual who relies on his own thinking, who does not place the beliefs of others before the functioning of his own mind. Here, it is most fully represented by Roark.

second-hander an individual who places the beliefs of others above the functioning of his own mind, whether as a follower or a rebel. Here, it is exemplified by Keating, Toohey, and, in one form or another, all of the novel's negative characters.

benevolent universe premise Ayn Rand's belief that the world is open to the achievement of values and happiness by good men and only by good men. Here, it is embodied in the life and ultimate success of Howard Roark.

malevolent universe premise the opposite of the benevolent universe premise. The view that the good have no chance in the world and that evil has the ultimate power. Here, it is the mistaken premise held by Dominique Francon.

totalitarianism a political system in which the government has full or *total* control over the life of the individual, who has no rights. It is the logical application to politics and economics of the collectivist view that an individual exists solely to serve society. Here, it is the theory of government advocated by Ellsworth Toohey.

Fascism a nationalistic type of collectivist dictatorship in which the individual is subordinate to the country or nation, as in Nazi Germany or Italy under Mussolini.

Communism a type of collectivist dictatorship in which the individual is subordinate to the needs of the poor or the working class, as in the Soviet Union. Here, the theory is advocated by Ellsworth Toohey.

CHARACTER ANALYSES

Howard Roark

Roark is a brilliant young architect of the modern school, whose bold and innovative designs are rejected by large segments of society. Although Ayn Rand does not base Roark's life on the specific events of Frank Lloyd Wright's life, Roark does possess many of the qualities and face many of the obstacles that the great, real-life, American modernist did.

Like Wright (1869–1959), Roark is fiercely independent. He believes in the merit of his revolutionary designs and has the courage to stand for them in the face of an antagonistic society. He is presented as the author's version of an ideal man—one who embodies the virtues of Ayn Rand's Objectivist philosophy. Roark is the antithesis of contemporary belief that an individual is molded by social forces. He is not the product of his upbringing, his economic class, his family, his religious training, or his social background. He is a product of the choices he has made. Roark is an example of *free will*—the theory that an individual has the power, by virtue of the choices he makes, to control the outcome of his own life. A man's thinking and values are not controlled by God or the fates or society or any external factor—but solely by his own choice. Others (like Keating) may choose to submit, but Roark will not. He is his own man.

Because Roark is his own man from the beginning, there is no change in the essence of Roark's character. He learns a significant amount over the course of the story—about architecture, the "principle behind the Dean," and other matters—but his fundamental convictions remain untouched. The essence of his character is an unswerving devotion to his own thinking and judgment. Roark is like this from the first moment of the story to the last—and, most likely, he has been this way since early childhood. An independent man like Roark learns a great deal of content in his life—indeed, because of his commitment to the fullest use of his own mind, he is the only type of person who can. But his *method of functioning*, his devotion to autonomous thinking, does not change. Because Roark's method of functioning doesn't change, he is able to create and successfully fight for revolutionary designs.

His first-handed method is also the principle that explains Roark's integrity. Integrity, according to Ayn Rand, is commitment in action to one's own best thinking, to one's own mind. Integrity is the "practice what you preach" virtue—the principle that you must put into practical action the ideas you hold. But first, of course, you must hold ideas. Integrity requires a man to be a thinker. Howard Roark meets both of these requirements. He is a brilliant thinker *and* he acts on his thinking. He is not a hypocrite.

Further, Roark is a *selfish* man, in the positive sense that Ayn Rand means this. He is true to his values, to his convictions, to his thinking, to his mind, to his *self*. When the board of the Manhattan Bank Building wants to alter his design, Roark rejects the proposal for the new design, calling his behavior "the most selfish thing you've ever seen a man do." Despite being destitute, he gives up a lucrative, publicity-generating commission in order to stand by the integrity of his design—and he calls this "selfish." To be true to his self, a man must first have a self. He must think independently, he must judge, he must form values and he must act in pursuit of those values. He must never sacrifice them. This is exactly what Roark does: The integrity of his design is far more important to him than the money or recognition that will accrue from the commission. In remaining true to his values and judgment, Roark is true to the deepest core of his self. This is selfishness in its highest and best sense.

An important moral question that Ayn Rand seeks to answer in Roark's character concerns the relationship between the moral and the practical. Many people in real life—as well as Gail Wynand and Dominique Francon in the novel—believe that practical success requires a betrayal of an individual's moral principles. It is often said that to succeed one must "play the game," or conform to the practices of one's company or profession even if one finds them unethical. To hold to one's scruples, according to this way of thinking, results only in loss of job or income, in a failure of some form. But in *The Fountainhead*, Ayn Rand builds a convincing argument that this cynical view is false. Howard Roark, she shows, is both a moral man and a practical man. His strength of character is demonstrated throughout the story. He is fully committed to the artistic integrity of every one of his designs, and he takes a laborer's job in a granite quarry rather than compromise on the smallest detail of his building. Integrity means conscientious commitment, *in action*, to the principles held by your own mind—and Roark exemplifies this virtue consistently, including when faced with destitution. Further, he is also a practical man. Roark, above all other characters in the novel, is a can-do giant of supreme competence. He excels at every aspect of building—from design to construction—and by the novel's end, he has achieved a significant commercial success. He is now established, on his own terms, in the field of architecture. That Roark is both a moral and a practical individual should be clear. But the most original aspect of Ayn Rand's presentation of Roark is that he is practical *because* he is moral, that these two qualities exist in a causal relationship.

Roark's moral stature is based on his commitment to his own mind regarding all issues of his life. He recognizes that human beings must rely on their minds for survival—that where animals employ such characteristics as speed of foot, size, strength, claws and fangs, wings, and/or fur in order to survive, man cannot rely on these physical attributes. He must be a thinker to grow food, build houses, manufacture clothes, and perform the other creative actions necessary to prosper on earth. But the mind is an attribute of the individual; just as there is no group stomach to digest for men collectively, so there is no group mind to perform collective thinking. Each man must accept responsibility for his own thinking and his own survival; each must be sovereign in living by his own most conscientious judgment. If a man sincerely—in his most scrupulously honest judgment—believes a claim to be true, then he must hold to this belief even though all of society opposes him. To be a thinker means to go by the factual evidence of a case, not by the judgment of others. To be a thinker means that if a man recognizes the perfection of an architectural design, he must not compromise it merely because others oppose him. Such willingness to live by his own thinking is independence and integrity—this is virtue. When Roark stands by the integrity of his designs, he stands by his mind. This is what makes him a moral and a practical man. For it is by means of his mind—not by conformity to others—that Roark builds. It is only by the fullest use of his mind that he—or any individual who does productive work—succeeds. A human being learns from others, as Roark does from Cameron, but he can neither think for others nor permit others to think for him. Any productive activity—including the construction work performed by Roark's friend, Mike Donnigan—requires *understanding*. Constructive work of any kind is not achieved by blindly mimicking the actions of others. The activities of building and growing—creating food, houses, automobiles, medical cures, airplanes, and computers—are intellectual in nature. All successful living for human beings require commitment to the mind. Roark's buildings, his ultimate commercial success, and his happiness are a result of living by his own thinking. Successful living forbids man to betray his mind. To surrender one's judgment is to exist like Peter Keating, a form in which no success or happiness is possible. Moral virtue is a requirement of practical success, not a hindrance to it.

Dominique Francon

Dominique is Roark's lover and later his wife. An ardent idealist, she observes Greek sculpture, Roark's buildings, the music of Tchaikovsky and Rachmaninoff, and she understands the human potential. Dominique recognizes man's capacity for achievement, and this is the only thing she loves. Because she reveres man at his highest and best, she necessarily loathes most members of the human race, who fall below man's potential. When she sees the manipulative Peter Keatings, the power-hungry Ellsworth Tooheys, and the masses who prefer Keating's work to Roark's, it fills her with despair. Dominique believes that the majority of men have no interest in living up to man's highest nature, and that this unthinking herd wields the power in society. Dominique is consequently a philosophical pessimist, holding that the good have no chance in this world, that only the corrupt (Keating) and the evil (Toohey) will ultimately succeed. She is a major example in Ayn Rand's writing of what the author terms the *malevolent universe premise*, the belief that the world is closed to the aspirations of good men, that only evil holds power.

Because of Dominique's reverence for man's noblest and best, she must love Roark; but because of her pessimism, she must hold the despairing belief that he has no chance to succeed in a world utterly hostile to him. She joins forces with Toohey, in an attempt to wreck Roark's career, as an act of mercy killing. Roark must die at *her* hand— that of the one who loves him—rather than by the hand of a society that envies his greatness. "Let us say we are moles and we object to mountain peaks," she admonishes the court and gallery at the Stoddard trial, stating that the temple must be torn down in order to save it from the world, not the world from it.

Because of Dominique's fear that the world will destroy the noble men and works that she treasures, she refuses to pursue any values. Because the only worthwhile goals could never be reached, Dominique refuses to pursue any goals. She withdraws from active involvement in the world, pursuing neither career nor love, until the events of the story, over a period of years, convince her that Roark's benevolent universe premise is true. Only when she sees the good succeeding on its own terms, and the evil powerless to stop it, does she realize that she has been mistaken regarding the world. Then she is free to help Roark and take her place by his side.

It is important to understand that, despite the error of her pessimistic philosophy, Dominique is independent in the use of her mind. The obvious examples of her first-handed functioning are her evaluations regarding architecture. Dominique understands that, despite some positive qualities, her father's career is essentially phony and not worthy of admiration—and she is not reticent about stating her beliefs openly. She displays the same ruthless honesty regarding her father's protégé and eventual partner, Peter Keating. Her independent judgment is equally apparent in regard to positive architectural appraisal—for despite society's rejection of Henry Cameron and, later, Howard Roark, she understands that these outcasts are the greatest builders in the world. Perhaps the most telling piece of evidence supporting Dominique's first-handedness is her assessment of Ellsworth Toohey. Though society regards Toohey as a paragon of moral saintliness, Dominique recognizes him for what he is—a viciously evil power-seeker.

The less obvious example of Dominique's independence is how she changes her mind regarding her pessimistic worldview. She observes the lives of Howard Roark, Gail Wynand, Peter Keating, and Ellsworth Toohey. She sees that despite every obstacle that society places in Roark's path, it cannot stop him. She witnesses the life of Gail Wynand, observing that, in the end, Wynand's pandering brings him destruction, not joyous success. She sees that Keating's career does not merely collapse, but does so because of his lying manipulativeness, which leads to his public exposure as a fraud. She notes that Toohey's power-seeking is utterly defeated in the two major attempts of his life: He can neither gain control of Wynand's *Banner* nor prevent Roark's artistic and commercial success. Dominique observes that the facts of these men's lives contradict her belief that the good will inevitably fail and the evil triumph. Based on the facts, she changes her mind, realizing that Roark's benevolent assessment of life's possibilities is true and her own malevolent view is mistaken. Her ability to change a fundamental component of her worldview is both rare and a testimony to her independence. She is committed to the facts, to truth, to her mind's most honest judgment—not to the opinions of others. Dominique is a thinker. The willingness to think for herself is what enables her to change her life, and demonstrates that though independence is not a guarantee of arriving at the truth, it provides an individual with a self-regulating method of correcting her errors.

Gail Wynand

Wynand is a powerful publisher of vulgar tabloids that oppose everything Roark stands for. But he also, like Dominique, loves man's noblest achievements, and owns a private gallery of great artworks. Wynand is a man of mixed premises. He rules his private life by means of his own judgment; consequently, it is filled with the items and persons that he, not his public, values. He loves Dominique, Roark, Roark's buildings, the beautiful art filling his gallery. Nobody—not his mother, Ellsworth Toohey, his public—tells Wynand how to conduct his personal life. Only his own thinking does this. But in his professional life, he is an egregious panderer. *The Banner* does not represent *his* values and thinking, but that of the most vulgar tastes of society. Ironically, the paper does not truly become Wynand's until he defends Roark in the Cortlandt case; only then does *The Banner* reflect Wynand's standards and values.

The story of Gail Wynand is tragedy. He is a man with the mind, talent, and initiative to do great things, but he brings disaster on himself by means of his own errors. Growing up in the harsh slums of Hell's Kitchen in New York City, he makes a fatal error, holding that, in this world, a man either rules or is ruled, conquers or is conquered. He believes that the majority of human beings are corrupt dolts—a mindless herd—and that the only way for the few intelligent and competent individuals to survive is by gaining power. He gives the public what it wants, attaining wealth and political influence along the way. But he betrays his own mind in the process.

Wynand is a man of exalted values, who panders to the debased standards of the crowd. Ultimately, the contradiction destroys him. When he defends Roark in *The Banner*, his thinking for the first time governs his paper's policy. He writes brilliant editorials defending the lone geniuses who stood against the men of their times, great individuals who, though persecuted by their societies, were vindicated by posterity. For the first time, Wynand uses his paper to defend the noble ideals he treasures. But he miscalculates. Those to whom he panders cannot appreciate a noble ideal, and those who can appreciate a noble ideal have long since stopped taking Wynand seriously. The paper comes back unread. Wynand had thought he had power. He believed that his papers molded public opinion. Bitterly, he discovers that his papers never belonged to him, but to the crowd—and that public opinion dictated his policies, not vice versa. Wynand discovers belatedly that, in seeking power, a man delivers himself to the very individuals he seeks to rule. He learns that a ruler must placate those ruled, and that his life is then dominated by the values of his subjects. If a ruler attempts to follow his own conscience—if he decides to flout the wishes of the herd—then the herd turns on him, throwing off his "authority" and turning to another. Wynand discovers that a power-seeker has no power—and that his own life was based on a lie.

Peter Keating

Keating is a conformist. He surrenders his judgment and allows other people to dominate his life. In this regard, he is the story's foil, a contrast to its hero, Roark. Everything that Keating does is done under the influence of others. He becomes an architect (although he would prefer the career of a painter), because his mother chooses it. He marries Dominique (although he loves Catherine Halsey), because Dominique's grace and beauty impress other people. In all the important decisions of his life, Keating gives up his own values because other people disapprove of them. Keating lacks the strength of character necessary to stand on his own judgment.

An aggressive social climber, Keating desires prestige above all else. Because Keating attempts to rise to the position of partner in the country's most prestigious firm—and because he uses any means necessary to attain this end, including flattery, deceit, and, in the case of Lucius Heyer, near-murder—he is conventionally thought of as selfish. But Ayn Rand presents a revolutionary analysis of such a status-seeker's nature. Peter Keating, she says, is self*less*. He sacrifices the things that he wants in order to please others. He surrenders his own loves and values in an attempt to win social approval. He relinquishes autonomy and permits others to dominate his life. Ayn Rand argues that in order to be selfish a man must be true to his *self*—and that the self is fundamentally a man's values along with the thinking he does to form them.

The meaning of the novel can be expressed in two words: judgment and values. A man must live by his own judgment and form his own values. He needs to understand that this is the sole means to the attainment of happiness. To yield on these fundamentals is to betray the self, it is to surrender the essence of what makes an individual uniquely and distinctively himself. Peter Keating surrenders his self in this way, and this is why, inevitably, he ends an empty shell of a man. If a man surrenders the things and/or persons he loves, then he will not achieve happiness. But Ayn Rand points out something deeper: If he abdicates his judgment, then he surrenders the very part of him with which he can experience happiness—his self. This is the meaning of Keating's life. He is selfless in a literal sense—he is without self.

Ellsworth Toohey

Toohey is a power-seeker. In various ways, he attempts to gain control over the lives of other men. At the personal level, he acquires a legion of followers who blindly obey his every command. Toohey deceives his victims by posturing as a humanitarian, but the code he preaches—that of self-sacrifice—is utterly destructive. Under the guise of offering spiritual guidance, Toohey convinces his followers to give up the things most important in their lives—their values. He tells them that virtue lies in selflessness, in the renunciation of personal desires, and that they must exist for the sake of others. He succeeds with a number of weak-willed individuals, who then surrender the things and persons most precious to them. But when a man gives up his values, he necessarily gives up that with which he formed them—his own thinking. His life is then empty, devoid of meaning and purpose, and he is incapable of internal direction. He needs external guidance. Toohey is never too busy to give them his full attention; he is always there to tell them what to do.

At the personal level, Toohey is a cult leader of a type such as Jim Jones, David Koresh, and Sun Myung Moon. He gains a private army of unquestioning followers, some of whom occupy positions of authority. He controls the souls of various government bureaucrats, of numerous Wynand employees and of millionaires like Hopton Stoddard and Mitchell Layton. It is through and by means of his victims that Toohey—like a virus—gains survival. Because he creates and contributes nothing, Toohey can exist only as a parasite. In this regard, he is the perfect antipode to Roark's creative genius.

But Toohey's power-seeking is not limited to his cult activities. He is the one character in the story who has political goals. Toohey seeks to establish a collectivist dictatorship in America. Because he is a

Marxist intellectual preaching communism to the masses, he desires to control editorial policy of the Wynand papers. With *The Banner* as a platform, Toohey hopes to spread the ideas necessary to establish a totalitarian state in America.

Toohey knows that a Fascist or Communist state requires a citizenry willing to obey. He can establish a dictatorship only if the majority of individuals are willing to give up personal autonomy—to surrender their minds to a leader. The Roarks of the world will not do it. But the Keatings will—in exchange for approval. Toohey understands that Keating, in order to be liked, will yield his thinking and values to others. Just as Keating fawns over professors, employers, critics—anyone in authority—so he will toady to the political leaders. Toohey's conclusion is simple: his plan requires many Keatings and no Roarks. This is the two-pronged goal that he attempts to reach: destroy the independent thinkers like Roark, and, by convincing individuals to surrender their judgment and values, turn them into followers like Keating. A dictator requires a flock of sheep; he cannot hold power over a citizenry of independent men.

Toohey has a clear vision of his role in the collectivist state. He himself is not the brute of physical force who gains dominance by unleashing a reign of terror. His role, rather, is to be the intellectual advisor behind the throne. The brute will hold physical power over the masses, and Toohey will hold spiritual power over the brute. Toohey is a behind-the-scenes puppet master, who surreptitiously wields the real power—and this will be his place in the totalitarian state he seeks.

Henry Cameron

Cameron is more than Roark's employer and architectural teacher. As mentor, he is the closest thing to a father that Roark has. Cameron is a brilliant and innovative thinker. As a fictional example of an early modern designer who is among the first to build skyscrapers, he is similar to the real-life American architect, Louis Sullivan (1856–1924). Cameron stands for the great innovators rejected by society. His genius is repudiated, and he dies a commercial failure. His struggle against a society closed to his revolutionary ideas is representative of many great freethinkers of history. Socrates, Galileo, Darwin, the Wright brothers, and many more were rejected, even persecuted, for the bold daring of the new truths they presented, and so it is with Cameron. Roark reveres

Cameron because of the older man's genius, his independent thinking, and his lifelong crusade for modern architecture, despite the price he must pay.

Further, Cameron, though bitter, is a profoundly benevolent figure in Roark's life. After three years of rejection by faculty members and administrators at Stanton Institute, Roark finds a man who, by one glance at his drawings, recognizes him as a budding genius. Cameron, the crusty curmudgeon, takes Roark into his charge and devotes himself to nurturing the precious talent with which he has been entrusted. Even on his deathbed, Cameron continues to mentor his protégé, instructing him to watch carefully the latest developments of the light metals and plastic industries, exhorting him to discover the new forms of building made possible by the technological advances. Though a commercial failure, Cameron is more than a moral and artistic success. Through the triumph of his (symbolically) adopted son, Roark, he helps ensure the final victory for his architectural principles.

Steven Mallory

Mallory is a brilliant young sculptor who becomes a close friend of Roark's. His work demonstrates an exalted view of the human potential. He sculpts figures of man the hero, capable of achievement. Roark understands that Mallory is the best sculptor there is. "Your figures are not what men are, but what men could be—and should be," Roark tells Mallory. "Because your figures are more devoid of contempt for humanity than any work I've ever seen. Because you have a magnificent respect for the human being. Because your figures are the heroic in man."

But when Roark meets him, Mallory is already cynical and embittered, disillusioned by rejection. Mallory, at this time, is a younger version of Henry Cameron, a brilliant innovator, whose work differs sharply from conventional standards, causing him to be rejected by most of society. Like Cameron, Mallory is loyal to his ideas and will not compromise. But also like Cameron, and unlike Roark, Mallory is affected by rejection. Although independent in thought and action, he is still tied to the beliefs of others at an emotional level; their repudiation hurts him, angers him, and rankles within his soul, leaving him bitter. Mallory is not as independent as Roark, and is on his way to alcoholism and despair. But if, symbolically, Cameron is Roark's father, then Mallory is his younger brother. It is too late for Roark's undiluted independence to have a positive impact in Cameron's life, but not in

Mallory's. Roark's character and conduct are an inspiration to Mallory, helping him realize that a man's values and ideals are the most important elements in life, not the beliefs of others.

Austen Heller

Heller, a man with individualistic beliefs, is a columnist for a dignified paper not at all like Wynand's tabloids. He knows nothing about architecture, but he knows what he likes—and he hires Roark to build a private home. Heller is a man who trusts his own judgment. Roark, after all, is not in private practice when Heller hires him—he is a mere employee in the office of John Erik Snyte. Although Roark as of yet has no professional credentials, Heller hires him on the sole basis of his sketch of the proposed house. The merit of Roark's design is the only credential that Heller requires.

Heller's character is demonstrated by means of several important details. The first is that he will not give a penny to charity. The second is that he gives more money than he can afford to help political prisoners around the globe. Heller refuses to contribute to charity because he believes that this merely furthers financial dependence and is, therefore, not in the recipient's self-interest. His generous aid to political prisoners is consistent with this. Political prisoners have committed no criminal actions. Their only "wrongdoing" is their commitment to political freedom and to free speech in a dictatorship. These are freethinking individuals with the courage to stand up for their ideals though it is unpopular, even dangerous to do so, in their societies. Heller is a consistent supporter of independence and, for this reason, is a friend and ally of Roark.

Mike Donnigan

Though a relatively minor figure in the novel, Mike's character dramatizes a significant point in Rand's philosophy. Mike is a construction worker, an electrician, who both admires competence and recognizes Roark's. Their mutual love of construction is the bond that unites them. Mike is not a genius; he is a man of more modest intelligence than Roark. But he knows buildings—and he sees with his own eyes and understands with his own mind. Mike recognizes that the buildings of Guy Francon, Ralston Holcolmbe, and Peter Keating are seriously flawed; the adulation these men receive from society does not alter Mike's judgment. He also recognizes that the buildings of Henry Cameron and Howard Roark are masterpieces, and society's repudiation of them cannot change his mind.

Mike's character shows independence is not a matter of a person's intelligence, but rather, of how he chooses to use it. Ellsworth Toohey possesses greater mindpower than does Mike, but Toohey's mind is employed in an utterly-dependent manner—devoted to flattering, deceiving, and manipulating others in order to control their souls. Mike's mind is not given to other people, but rather, to building. He may not be a genius, but within the scale of his own concerns, Mike is an independent thinker. In his combination of ordinary intelligence and first-handed method, Mike can be thought of as Everyman at his best. His autonomous functioning is not merely the basis of his bond with Roark, but further demonstrates that moral character is not a question of intelligence but of its use.

Kent Lansing

Lansing is a salesman with a rare appreciation of artistic genius and an even rarer willingness to fight for it. He is a member of the board formed to build the Aquitania Hotel, a luxury establishment on Central Park South. Lansing recognizes Roark's extraordinary talent, even though at this early point of Roark's career, his major projects have been limited to the Enright House and the Cord Building. Lansing's supreme virtue is a stubborn commitment to fight for his values, an indomitable doggedness that enables him to triumph over a multitude of obstacles, across a period of years, to construct the Aquitania as he desires it. When construction of the hotel is stopped due to a series of lawsuits, Lansing vows to win legal control of the project, and retain Roark to complete it. Promising to finish it, no matter the length of time required, Lansing advises Roark, "I won't tell you to be patient. Men like you and me would not survive beyond their first fifteen years if they did not acquire the patience of a Chinese executioner. And the hide of a battleship." Though it takes five years to successfully resolve the legal disputes, Lansing perseveres. He keeps his word, and Roark eventually completes the hotel.

Lansing describes himself as a salesman, and shows Roark the value of a middleman. He says that Roark could explain to the board the proper reasons for hiring him much more effectively than anyone else.

But the board's members will not listen to him; they will reject as self-ishly prejudicial any remarks on his hiring that Roark makes. Lansing points out that people often find it easier to pass judgment on a man rather than on an idea, even though it is both illogical and unjust to judge a man without considering the content of his thinking. Lansing explains to Roark the reasons for this. He says that to understand and evaluate a man's thinking requires firm principles or standards which, tragically, most people lack. They do not possess carefully thought-out and tested principles of their own; they merely allow themselves to be buffeted on serious issues by the important people in their lives. In short, most people are followers and are too afraid to stand on their own. They will not see the truth of the new ideas created by an innovator like Roark. They need to hear it from others. They need to hear it from a middleman—and the more middlemen the better. Because men generally fear independence, a revolutionary thinker like Roark needs a few rare men like Lansing to both recognize and fight for the merit of his work. Lansing plays an invaluable role in Roark's life. He understands the brilliance of Roark's creative work and will take on any obstacle to procure a Roark design for his hotel. In the struggle that Lansing fights and wins, he demonstrates that independence and integrity are not the exclusive prerogative of the creative artist, but are sometimes possessed by the middleman, as well.

Roger Enright

Enright is a tough, hard-bitten entrepreneur who began his career as a coal miner in Pennsylvania and who earned his fortune through years of prodigious effort. But Enright is more than a self-made multi-millionaire. His method of conducting business is strikingly innovative. He branches out into many fields, ranging from the oil business to publishing, from restaurants to the manufacture of refrigerators. Before entering a field, Enright studies it assiduously, gaining a wealth of information. Then he proceeds to overturn every element of accepted wisdom in the industry, acting as though he had never heard of what had previously been done. Some of his innovative ventures fail, though many succeed, and he continues to run them all "with ferocious energy," working twelve hours a day.

Enright's independence extends to other aspects of his life, as well. He refuses to buy or sell stock. He owns his fortune single-handed, "as simply as if he carried all his cash in his pocket." When he decides to construct a building, Enright searches for the proper architect for six months, then hires Roark at the end of a 30-minute interview. Enright tells Roark not to bother explaining the building to him, because he has no abstract ideals or principles, and no capacity to learn any. He says that he simply goes by what he likes, "But I do know what I like." Enright—like Lansing—not only knows what he wants, but is willing to break all established conventions to accomplish it. It is a surprise neither that Enright attends Roark's trial for the Cortlandt dynamiting, sitting with Roark's other friends, nor that he buys from the government the site, the plans, and the ruins of Cortlandt, then hires Roark to build it in exact accordance with Roark's original design. Enright is the fictional epitome of an independent entrepreneur who rises from the bottom by means of his own talent and work ethic. As such, it is natural that he would admire, hire, and befriend Roark.

Guy Francon

Guy Francon is a mediocre architect who attains commercial success by consummate mastery of the social graces. Handsome, well-groomed, impeccably dressed, charming, and debonair, Francon wines and dines prospective clients at New York's most exclusive restaurants. He offers the public impressive Greek columns and showy white marble fronts; his work is all glitter and no substance. He is a phony and a second-hander. His success is based on two factors: He copies from the Classical designers, and he impresses customers with suave urbanity. He imitates and receives undeserved acclaim; this is his career. But despite these serious flaws, Francon possesses good qualities that enable him to attain a level of happiness in the end.

Francon's virtues are that beauty, charm, and fine attire are good things—and though Francon is an egregious imitator, at least he has the good judgment to copy from the geniuses of Classical Greece. He is a conformist but chooses to mimic the best of what society believes. But above all, of all the second-handers, Francon is the least antagonistic to Roark. Though he does not approve of the Stoddard Temple, he refuses to testify at the trial because, says Dominique, "he did not think we were behaving like gentlemen." Critically, Francon not only loves his daughter, he does so for the right reason—for her unconquerable soul. Whenever he thinks he should hate her, his mind reverts involuntarily to an incident of her childhood in which she leaped an obstacle he had thought too high for her. It is engraved in his memory as the greatest illustration of freedom and ecstasy he has ever witnessed—and at some unspoken level of emotion he realizes what this says about Dominique's spirit. Because of this, he realizes that Roark is the right man for her and is happy. Despite the scandalized embarrassment of his friends, Guy Francon sits with Roark's allies at the Cortlandt trial.

Francon's redeeming characteristic is his genuine love for his daughter's best qualities. This means that in spite of the insincere nature of his career, there remains in Francon's soul one last, unbetrayed element, committed to a life of achievement and happiness.

Catherine Halsey

Catherine Halsey is a victim of Ellsworth Toohey and a perfect example of Toohey's ghastly method of power-seeking. Early in the story, Katie is a sincere, good-natured girl, genuinely in love with Peter Keating. Though she had not been a great high school student, she planned on going to college, a goal supported by Keating but not by Toohey, her uncle. She is wishy-washy regarding this dream and allows Toohey to talk her out of it.

The one consuming passion of Katie's life is her love for Keating. But her uncle works hard to convince Keating to woo Dominique, not Katie, knowing that if his scheme succeeds, he will have reached two goals at once: He will have emptied Keating's soul of its last personal value and deprived Katie's soul of its only value. The lives of both will then be devoid of meaning, love, and passion. Both will be internally empty vessels, lost at sea and floundering, existing in painful misery, crying for a leader to guide them. This is exactly what happens. Keating loves Katie but abandons her for a showcase wife in the person of Dominique Francon. Keating's betrayal is a crushing blow to Katie. Toohey succeeds in conquering both of their souls. Katie, in empty despair, turns to the altruistic creed of her uncle, becoming, in effect, a miniature version of Toohey, seeking spiritual power over the poor individuals to whom she ministers as a social worker.

When Keating meets Katie by chance on the streets of New York, years after his abandonment of her, she is a bustling Washington bureaucrat, who exists to give orders, "not big orders or cruel orders; just mean little ones—about plumbing and disinfectants." She is neither angry, hurt, nor embarrassed at their meeting. She simply takes unstrained control of their time together, tells him what he will eat, and listens in amused tolerance to his heartbreaking admission that marrying her was the only thing he had ever wanted to do. Katie is Toohey writ small: She possesses no values or personal loves—she considers them "self-ish"—only a desire to control small matters in the lives of weak people who are either unable or unwilling to control their own lives. As a consequence of possessing a soul devoid of personal values, she is an unfeeling automaton who bustles through her days in cold controlling efficiency.

As a chilling victim of Toohey's power lust, Katie serves to illustrate an important aspect of Ayn Rand's philosophy. Her sweetness, innocence, and good nature are inadequate to protect her from Toohey's evil. She was a conventional person, dutifully following her family and her uncle, not too ambitious, not committed to living by her own judgment or pursuing her own dreams. Her lack of independence—her unwillingness to bear the responsibility of sustained, self-initiated thought—costs her the loss of her soul. An uncritical emotional sweetness of disposition is insufficient to gain a person happiness or to protect her against evil. She needs to use her own mind to think for herself. A lack of independent thinking is what dooms Katie's attempt to gain love and happiness.

Lois Cook

Lois Cook is an outstanding example of the meaning of *nonconformity*. She defies social belief in beauty, attractive living quarters, and even personal hygiene. In this regard, she is far worse than Guy Francon, for he uncritically follows the best of society's norms where Cook rebels against them. Worse than this is her incoherent style of writing. She rebels against grammar, meaning, and intelligibility. Her book has no discernible meaning, yet she postures as a profound thinker. All she needs is a few power-seeking critics like Ellsworth Toohey to sing the praises of her books, and the followers like Keating—too timid to form their own judgments—will accept Toohey's evaluations.

Lois Cook is not merely a second-hander whose life is dominated by the people against whose values she rebels. She is an example of *nihilism*—a desire to destroy the best that human society has to offer. She doesn't fight against vulgar tabloids, corrupt politicians, widespread illiteracy, or any of society's ills. Instead she attacks cleanliness, beauty, and literary intelligibility—the best of men's values. As one of Toohey's more important protégés, Lois Cook is as committed to destruction as is her leader.

Gus Webb

Gus Webb is an avant-garde architect, another of Toohey's followers, whose buildings are mere collections of boxes piled on one another. He lacks all standards of design, even borrowed ones; his stacks of boxes disregard all questions of a building's function, its needs, its practical requirements. Like Lois Cook, Webb is a nihilist, a rebel against the best of other men's values. He doesn't bathe, he delights in uttering obscenities to well-bred ladies he passes in the streets, and his personality is that of a vulgar lout. He is a second-hander whose life is ruled by the middle-class individuals he loathes and defies.

Webb speaks of "the movement" and of the "workers' revolution"; his response to Roark's dynamiting of Cortlandt is revealing: "I wish he'd blasted it when it was full of people—a few children blown to pieces—then you'd have something. Then I'd love it. The movement could use it." Gus Webb is a fictional forerunner of the New Left of the 1960s. Whereas the Old Left of the 1930s, represented by Toohey, was a movement of cultured, highly educated intellectuals, the New Left scorned theory and intellect, opting instead for political activism. At a political level, Webb's character represents a prediction by Rand: Because Marxism stands for totalitarian dictatorship and suppression of the free-thinking mind, it must necessarily lose all vestiges of cultured intellectuality. It must degenerate into a movement of unbathed, drug-addicted activists who physically occupy classrooms and shut down the educational process. In the character of Gus Webb, Ayn Rand predicted the existence and nature of the New Left twenty-five years before it appeared on the American cultural scene in the late 1960s.

CRITICAL ESSAYS

The Literary Integration of
The Fountainhead

The manner in which Ayn Rand integrates the theme of *The Fountainhead* with other literary elements is important. The theme of *The Fountainhead* is the contrast of, and conflict between, persons of independent functioning and those of dependent functioning. The plot is an ideal vehicle by which to present this theme.

The essence of the plot line is an innovative modern architect struggling against a society indifferent or hostile to his revolutionary ideas. The innovative architect is an independent thinker. Those who reject him are dependent persons who, in one form or another, allow the thinking of others to dominate their lives. They are unable or unwilling to see the truth of the new ideas. Note that it is impossible to discuss the novel's plot without introducing its theme. The two are inextricably intertwined, which can be seen by analyzing the specific men who reject Roark. These men fall into three types and each is a variation on the theme of psychological dependence.

The first type is the *traditionalists*—those so blindly wedded to the thinking of the past that they cannot see the truth of any new ideas. History abounds with examples of traditionalists: those who rejected Copernicus' heliocentric theory because of their commitment to the older geocentric view; those who could not see the truth of Darwin's theory of evolution because of their Fundamentalist religious beliefs; those who rejected Fulton's steamboat because their prior experience was limited to sail. Among those opposed to Cameron and Roark are many of this same type. The Dean of Stanton Institute believes that all truths of architecture were discovered by the builders of the past; modern architects can only copy their achievements. Guy Francon imitates the designs of the Classical period and Ralston Holcolmbe of the Renaissance. The gradual acceptance of Henry Cameron's innovations is thwarted by the Columbian Exposition of 1893. The Rome of two thousand years ago rises on the shores of Lake Michigan, precipitating a rebirth of Classicism in America, closing the public's mind to Cameron's ideas. "A young country had watched him on his way, had wondered, had begun to accept the new grandeur of his work. A country flung two thousand years back in an orgy of Classicism could find no place for him and no use." The traditionalists believe that the age of an idea—particularly its old age—is a conclusive factor certifying its truth. To them, truth is not a relationship between an idea and the facts, but between an idea and their ancestors. They are blinded to the present by their commitment to the past. This is why the Dean, Guy Francon, and Ralston Holcolmbe are unable to recognize the merits of Cameron's and Roark's innovations.

The second type of men who reject Roark are the *conformists*—those who blindly accept the ideas of their peers. Many such individuals can be found in life. Most people who hold religious convictions—be they Catholics, Protestants, Jews, or Muslims—do not study comparative religion, but simply accept the beliefs of their families. Some individuals surrender their career preference or romantic choice in order to meet their parents' expectations. Others may know the dangers of drug use but, to please their friends, indulge nevertheless. Similarly, the universe of *The Fountainhead* is populated with such characters. Numerous individuals reject Roark's ideas solely because his thinking clashes with the beliefs of those around them. For example, Robert Mundy, a self-made man who grew up in poverty in Georgia, is one such person. Mundy asks Roark to build him a southern-style plantation house, not because he values it, but because it is a symbol of the aristocrats who ridiculed him as a young man. Though Roark explains patiently that such a house would not stand for his own struggle and values, but for the values of his tormentors, Mundy refuses to acknowledge Roark's point; he wants the plantation house because others valued it. Mrs. Wayne Wilmot of Long Island wants to hire Roark so that she can tell her friends she has Austen Heller's architect. She wants an English Tudor home because of "the picture post cards she had seen, [and] the novels of country squires she had read." Members of the board of the Janss-Stuart Real Estate Company refuse Roark's design because "no one has ever built anything like it." John Erik Snyte, an architect for whom Roark briefly works, differs from Guy Francon's commitment to the Classical style. Snyte is not wedded to any specific school of design; he cheerfully gives the public whatever style it wants. Mostly, there is Peter Keating, who is driven by an almost uncontrollable urge to impress others and win acclaim. Keating seeks prestige, and his method is to fawn over others, especially those in authority, and spout back to them their own ideas. He is an intellectual chameleon, who takes on the beliefs of others in order to gain their approval. Keating even expresses his policy as a formal principle, when he states to Roark, "Always be what people want you to be. Then you've got them where you want them." Keating's code is the perfect expression of a conformist's soul—putting the beliefs of others above and before the functioning of his own mind. Such an unthinking mentality is incapable of recognizing the genius of Roark's work—or that of any other innovator.

The third and last type of men who reject Roark are the *socialists*—those committed to the principle that it is an individual's unchosen moral obligation to serve society, and to the political-economic implementation of this belief. In real life examples of socialist principles include the contemporary American welfare state that compels productive individuals to support the nonproductive. Various socialist states in Europe and around the globe provide a similar, though much more extreme, example. Finally, Communism and Fascism—the fullest, most consistent political expressions of an individual's duty to selflessly serve society—still exist as ideologies and as forms of government in some countries. In *The Fountainhead*, Ellsworth Toohey is the distilled essence of such a socialist mentality. Toohey preaches socialism relentlessly in his column, "One Small Voice," and in every other forum open to him. He believes individuals are obligated to sacrifice for society, that a country requires a dictatorial government to coercively enforce those obligations, and that the most creative and productive should be compelled to serve those less so. In Toohey's world there is no room for those who will not obey. Independent thinkers will either be broken or eliminated. No Howard Roarks will be tolerated. Toohey makes clear his views in a "confession" speech to Peter Keating near the novel's end. In answer to Keating's question, "Why do you want to kill Howard?" Toohey minces no words. He doesn't want Roark dead, he says, but alive in a cell where he will finally be forced to obey. "They'll push him, if he doesn't move fast enough, and they'll slap his face when they feel like it, and they'll beat him with rubber hose if he doesn't obey. And he'll obey. He'll take orders. *He'll take orders!*" Toohey, the advocate of a socialist dictatorship, must break the spirit of freethinkers like Roark.

The three types of persons who reject Roark—the traditionalists, the conformists, and the socialists—are variations on the theme of second-handedness. None are independent thinkers; all permit others to dominate their lives in some form. The traditionalists copy the thinking of their ancestors; the conformists copy the thinking of their contemporaries; the socialists seek to extirpate thinking in their contemporaries, transforming them into blind followers of the political leadership. The traditionalists and conformists are followers of others; the socialists desire to rule others, but in ruling must placate the crowd to keep it from rising against them. All copy from or cater to others. All look to society for the fundamentals of their existences; all are psychologically dependent on other people. Not one is willing to wrest his mind from the thrall of other men, to look at nature, to think and judge independently, to perform creative work. They are all opposite to Roark in cognitive functioning; in one form or another, they are all threatened by him; and all reject his originality and autonomy. Inexorably, all three types line up against Roark as his opponents.

The novel's story line is Roark's quest to build his type of buildings. Roark is opposed by persons such as the Dean, Guy Francon, Ralston Holcolmbe, John Erik Snyte, Peter Keating, and Ellsworth Toohey in a conflict pitting an independent thinker against every conceivable type of psychological dependent. Ayn Rand's theme is perfectly expressed by her story. This integration of literary elements can be further seen by examining the book's characters, both major and minor. Each character is a carefully etched variation on the book's theme. In some cases, this is fairly obvious; in others, it is not obvious at all.

Howard Roark is an exemplar of the creative mind. He is more than an independent thinker; he is a genius. He is a fictional example of the greatest minds of history, the exalted thinkers who discovered important new truths only to be rejected by society. The Wright Brothers were scoffed at, Robert Fulton was ridiculed, and Louis Pasteur was bitterly denounced. In the field of architecture, Modernist designers like Louis Sullivan and Frank Lloyd Wright fought a decades-long struggle to win acceptance for their new ideas. The histories of science, philosophy, and art are filled with examples of innovative thinkers whose ideas were rejected by the men of their times. Roark's character, his struggle and triumph, are Ayn Rand's impassioned tribute to the great freethinkers who have carried mankind forward on their shoulders, have often met hysterical opposition, and have rarely received the recognition they deserve. The character of Howard Roark holds a place in the history of world literature—along with such giants as Antigone and Dr. Stockman in Ibsen's *An Enemy of the People*—as a paragon of human independence.

Keating and Toohey are also obvious variations on the novel's theme. Keating is a status seeker, a man so afraid to risk social disapproval that he willingly surrenders his mind to others. He is an example of the pitiable nature of conformity—the motives, the behavior, the consequences, resulting in a man whose soul is voluntarily turned over to society. Despite an endless series of malicious actions, Keating is ultimately a pathetic person, not an evil one, and the pathos contains a warning: A man betrays his soul at his own peril. The person who is dependent on social approval for his self-esteem sacrifices his values and his mind, and necessarily ends as an empty shell of a man. Keating, like the main character in Sinclair Lewis' *Babbitt*, is a superb literary example of conformity, of one form of dependence on others.

Power-seeking is another such form. In the character of Ellsworth Toohey, Ayn Rand makes important points regarding the nature of the man who pursues power over other men. Conventionally, cult leaders and political dictators have not been viewed as weak psychological dependents, but as the opposite—as strong individuals whose control over others is a logical expression of their strength. The German philosopher Friedrich Nietzsche is one famous example of a man who glorifies the conqueror's over-brimming strength and vitality—and, more generally, dictators are referred to as "political strongmen." Civilized men, prior to Ayn Rand, had rejected the belief that there is glory in conquest, but still believed it to represent strength. In the characters of Roark and Toohey, Ayn Rand shows that this view is false. Roark is a strong man—one willing to accept the responsibilities of independent thinking. He looks at facts, he judges, he stands on his own convictions regardless of the beliefs of the crowd. Because Roark is a thinker, he is not tied to social approval. He looks to the outer world, to nature, for truth, and consequently, he is able to build. This man, the one who conquers nature, is the man with power. This is human strength.

But Roark is everything that Toohey is not. Toohey is terrified of independent judgment; he feels inadequate to confront nature directly. He is intelligent enough to realize that man's survival requires first-handed thinking. "A sublime achievement, isn't it," he says to Dominique, gazing at the city. "And it is said that but for the spirit of a dozen men, here and there down the ages, but for a dozen men—less, perhaps—none of this would have been possible." The minor point is that though Toohey recognizes Roark to be one of those men, he nevertheless seeks his destruction. The major point is that though he identifies the need of independent thought, he refuses to change his methods. He is unwilling to face the immutable world of nature that cannot be bent to his wishes. Rather, he confines himself to the world of men, to craven creatures like Peter Keating who can be molded to suit his desires. In spite of his understanding of man's survival requirements, he refuses to devote his intelligence to the conquest of nature; instead, he commits it to the conquest of men. Having given up all attempts at an independent life, he exists solely as a parasite; he survives as a virus does, by invading the tissue of healthy organisms. He needs the Keatings far more than they need him, because they can build after a fashion, but Toohey can construct nothing. The Keatings receive approval from Toohey, but Toohey gains survival from his followers. He is the most abjectly dependent creature inhabiting the universe of *The Fountainhead*.

Wynand and Dominique are also variations on the novel's theme, though in a form much less readily discernible. Wynand is a mixed case. A commonly held belief in our society says that, "there is no black and white, all are shades of gray." The characters in *The Fountainhead* show clearly that Ayn Rand disagrees with this view. Roark, Keating, and Toohey are not blends of independence and dependence, of good and evil. Rather, each is utterly consistent, fully one or the other. Roark is fully independent, possessing no elements of second-handedness. Toohey and Keating, on the other hand, are abject second-handers with no independent qualities. Wynand is the character who represents a mixture of incompatible elements. He is partly first-handed in his functioning but also partly second-handed. In his person, Rand shows the disastrous consequences of any attempt to mix logically contradictory qualities.

In his private life, Wynand lives by his own judgment. Because he is an idealist who reveres human excellence, his personal life is filled with examples of man's achievements. He recognizes Roark's genius, and commissions him to design major buildings. Likewise, he recognizes Roark's integrity, and embraces him as his dearest friend. Despite Dominique's errors, he identifies immediately her nobility of spirit and falls deeply in love with her. Finally, he fills his private art gallery with works of only the most exquisite beauty. Wynand's private life is lived in faithful accordance with his own exalted standards.

But his public life is an example of the most egregious pandering. *The Banner* is a lurid tabloid filled with loathsome values, directed toward the most vulgar tastes of the crowd, presenting none of Wynand's own high ideals. It is a double disgrace, for it is not only a yellow-press scandal sheet but is owned and published by a man of the most high-minded ideals. Ironically, *The Banner* becomes Wynand's paper only when he defends Roark's genius. He inevitably fails in his noble crusade because his readership has no interest in the ideals he defends, and sincere idealists can no longer take him seriously. Wynand allows the values of others to dictate his career, making it, in the end, impossible to get a hearing for his own values. His decades-long dependence on the standards of others makes it impossible to successfully defend his own. In the end, Wynand is defeated by his attempt to live a double life—and the tragic lesson of his character is that there is no middle ground between independence and dependence; there is no possibility of peaceful coexistence between these opposing methods of conducting one's life.

Where Wynand is a man whose independent functioning is undercut by an element of pandering, Dominique is a woman thoroughly independent but who makes a serious, though honest, error. Dominique is a thinker, a woman who sees with her own eyes and understands with her own mind. The beliefs of others do not influence her thinking. She recognizes that both her father and Keating are phony, second-rate architects despite their popular acclaim—and she understands the genius of Cameron and Roark, though most of society rejects them. She, preeminently among the characters, comprehends Toohey's evil, an identification unaffected by society's proclamations of his sainthood. But her first-hand method of functioning does not prevent her from making a serious error.

Dominique believes that virtue has no chance to succeed in a corrupt world, that great men like Roark are doomed to suffer the fate of Cameron, finishing as lonely outcasts. Phonies like Francon, manipulators like Keating, power-lusters like Toohey—these contemptible persons are the ones who succeed in the world. Roark, Dominique believes, is heading toward a tragic fate. Ayn Rand calls this pessimistic view of life the *malevolent universe premise*. Although Dominique's belief is grounded in the specific facts of her experience, her generalization is unwarranted. Ultimately, Roark does not merely succeed, he succeeds because he is a man of uncompromising principles. Keating does not merely fail, he fails because he sells his soul. Toohey does not merely fail in both his attempts to stop Roark and to control the Wynand papers; he fails because his corrosive evil has only the power to destroy, not the power to create. Dominique witnesses these events and, consequently, realizes her error. In the end, she understands that Roark is right: Only the good men can attain practical success, because only they possess the power to create. She thereby accepts what Rand calls the *benevolent universe premise*, which is the realization that the world is open to value achievement by the good men and only by the good men.

Because Dominique is a thinker, she is able to identify her error, change her mind and her actions, and achieve happiness. She makes an error in the content of her thinking, but because her method is first-handed, she is able to correct it. The lesson of her character is that independent thinking does not make a person infallible, but it does provide a self-correcting mechanism by means of which to identify and eradicate errors. Her character, too, is a variation on the theme of independence.

The same is true regarding many of the book's lesser characters. Henry Cameron and Steven Mallory are good examples. Cameron and Mallory are both innovative thinkers, creative geniuses whose new ideas are rejected by society. Both refuse to compromise, and each pays a price for his integrity. Both, in other words, are independent in thought and action. But both are hurt and angered by the unjust treatment they receive from society. Both remain true to their ideas, neither conforms—but Cameron becomes bitter and cynical and Mallory, when Roark meets him, is moving in that direction. Like Roark, they are uncompromising men of integrity; they, too, in thought and deed, will not betray their own minds. But unlike Roark, Cameron and Mallory permit society's rejection to fester at the emotional level. The rejection matters to them in a personal way, a way that goes beyond the harmful impact on their careers. Where Roark has integrated the virtue of independence throughout every aspect of his person—thought, action, *and* emotion—Cameron and Mallory have fallen short. Though admirable men, they possess a tragic flaw absent in Roark: they allow the beliefs of others to cause them emotional pain. Consequently, they do not live in the full state of joy and pride that their glorious achievements should provide. The undeserved suffering of these two great men is, at one level, an indictment of a tradition-bound society that rejects innovators. At a deeper level, their suffering is an exhortation to original thinkers not to permit the beliefs of others to hold power over them. These two heroes thereby represent one aspect of the theme: The virtue of independence must be assimilated into every aspect of a man's life, the emotional as well as the intellectual and the practical.

Austen Heller also needs to be understood as a variation on the novel's theme of independence. Heller is a journalist who stands for the same principles of limited government and political/economic freedom that animated the founding fathers of the United States. His writings defend the "inalienable rights" of the individual. Further, Heller will not contribute a penny to charity, but contributes more than he can afford to help political prisoners around the globe. He does not give to charities, because supporting non-working people encourages a form of dependence. He helps political prisoners, because in defending individual rights against the oppression of a dictator, they stand for political freedom, a form of independence. Heller is a carefully etched variation on the novel's theme of independence as a requirement of man's life.

Roger Enright is another good example of an independent hero. Enright is an entrepreneur, a man in business for himself. He started out as a coal miner in Pennsylvania, rising to his present fortune by his own talent and initiative. "On the way to the millions he now owned, no one had ever helped him. 'That,' he explained, 'is why no one has ever stood in my way.'" He is a self-made man, who has never sold a share of stock in any of his enterprises. Enright owns his entire fortune single-handed, "as simply as if he carried all his cash in his pocket." Before venturing into a field, he studies it for months, then proceeds as if he had never heard of the way things are generally done. He is an innovator, and though some of his ventures succeed and others fail, he continues to forge ahead with new ideas. Enright, the self-made man who rises from poverty by his own initiative, is a fictitious example of the kind of fiercely independent entrepreneur who flourishes in a free economy.

The novel's theme is also the essence of the negative characters. Take, for example, Hopton Stoddard, who hires Roark to build a Temple of the Human Spirit. Stoddard is a guilt-ridden businessman who has made a fortune, in part, through various shady deals. Seeking penance, he subscribes to Toohey's code of self-sacrifice and contributes to the causes Toohey recommends. In general, he is a slavish follower of Toohey. His last spark of independence is his insistence on building the temple. His quest for forgiveness has driven him to religion and, in desperation, he wishes to make God an offering. Toohey, an atheist and a socialist, wants Stoddard to build a home for sick children, but, for once, Stoddard refuses to obey. He is adamant—it must be a temple. Toohey finally agrees, knowing that the masterpiece Roark designs will be so unlike traditional places of worship that the public and Stoddard will be appalled. Toohey's main purpose is to make Roark notorious as an "enemy of religion." But a secondary gain is the way he can make the terrified Stoddard bear responsibility for the fiasco, and manipulate him into building the home for afflicted children. Toohey's scheme succeeds regarding Stoddard, whose last vestige of autonomous functioning is eliminated. He now follows Toohey unquestioningly in all moral issues. "In matters of the spirit he regarded Toohey upon earth somewhat as he expected to regard God in heaven." Stoddard's character illustrates that a guilt-ridden man is a prime candidate to accept a code of self-sacrifice, and to surrender his soul to the spiritual authorities who preach it. Toohey's approval assuages Stoddard's guilt, and so he kneels, he follows, he obeys.

All the minor characters obey in the way that Stoddard does. In various forms, all of these characters voluntarily surrender their minds to society, granting to others the status of master. Guy Francon, for example, is a phony. His impeccable manners, his elegant garb, his French vocabulary are all devices calculated to achieve one goal: to impress others. Other than his love for Dominique, Francon has no values of his own. His professional life is a series of actions catering to the tastes of the public. He is merely a servant. Society is his master.

Lois Cook is a different variation on psychological dependence. She is an avant-garde writer, composing in a "word salad" style, a series of incoherent sentences in which the words are related by sound and emotional association, not by an attempt to communicate meaning. Her goal, as stated by the expressionists and Dadaists of the early twentieth century, is to "shock the bourgeoisie." She is a nonconformist who attacks the values of others. Just as Cook's unintelligible writing style is a deliberate assault on the rules of grammar and meaning, so her slovenly personal habits are also calculated to shock society, whose members value beauty and grooming. As with a conformist like Guy Francon, Cook's life is dominated by the values of other people. Francon panders to the tastes of others; Lois Cook flouts them. But to both Francon and Cook, the standards of others is the ruling concern.

The foregoing analyses can be replicated with every character in the story. Each one is a distinctive variation on the principles of independence or dependence. Ayn Rand, in describing Roark's achievement at Monadnock Valley—the manner in which the individual houses constituting the resort are unique but similar—provides a fitting account of her own achievement: "There were many houses, they were small, they were cut off from one another, and no two of them were alike. But they were like variations on a single theme, like a symphony played by an inexhaustible imagination, and one could still hear the laughter of the force that had been let loose on them, as if that force had run, unrestrained, challenging itself to be spent, but had never reached its end." Each character in the story is, similarly, a variation on a single theme, created by an inexhaustible imagination.

The plot—the struggle of an innovative architect to win acceptance for his ideas against the entrenched beliefs of society—is a perfect vehicle to express the theme. Additionally, the specific antagonists who oppose the creator/hero—traditionalists, conformists, and socialists—are all variations on the theme of second-handedness, further dramatizing the novel's theme. Finally, each character—major and minor, positive and negative—is a distinctive variation on the theme. The overall result is a tightly integrated work of literature, expressing a profound thesis regarding human nature.

Ayn Rand's Writing Style

The subtlety of Ayn Rand's style can be understood by examining a representative scene. Near the end of Part One, Roark is offered the commission to design the Manhattan Bank Building. It is a major commission at a time when he needs it desperately, but the board wishes to alter his design. Roark, to whom the integrity of his design is far more important than money or recognition, refuses. The means by which Ayn Rand presents the scene is revealing.

The board presents Roark with an altered sketch of his building. The first thing Roark does is get up: "He had to stand. He concentrated on the effort of standing. It made the rest easier." He leans on the table with his right arm. When he answers, the men of the board cannot tell whether he is too calm or too emotional—but because his words move forward evenly, with neither anger nor excitement, they conclude he is calm, despite the fact that "the air in the room was not the air that vibrates to a calm voice." The board members also notice that Roark's demeanor and posture are normal; he is exhibiting no strange mannerisms, except that his right hand clings to the table's edge, and he moves the drawings with his left hand, as if his right is paralyzed. What is the significance of these details?

Notice that Ayn Rand chooses to narrate the scene through the eyes (and ears) of the board members. The reader gets only the sensory information available to the men in the room, seeing and hearing what they do. Ayn Rand does not tell the reader what emotions Roark is feeling. Instead, she shows the observational details that the reader would get were he sitting in the room, too. After all, an individual has no direct way of experiencing another person's emotions; all he can do is observe the sensory clues and infer. If a man's face is red, his eyes wild, and his voice loud, we can infer that he is angry. The readers of *The Fountainhead* discover a character's emotions the way they do it in real life: by inference from observational evidence.

Secondly, the members of the board are mistaken in their interpretation of Roark. They believe that, because Roark speaks softly and rationally, he is calm. But the factual evidence indicates otherwise. Why does Roark feel the need to stand? What is it that is made "easier" when he stands? Why does standing require an "effort"? Roark leans on his right arm, he refuses to move it, he turns pages with his left hand, looking like a man with one arm paralyzed. Why? Clearly, Roark experiences powerful emotion in this scene. His building may be compromised, his career is in jeopardy, and his commitment to his principles is tested. The disappointment, the pain, the anger at their stubborn, blind refusal to see and hear the truth so compellingly obvious to Roark is overwhelming. Roark struggles with the intensity of his feeling, struggles to keep his mind and his voice calm so that he can reason with the men, so that he can show them the brilliant lucidity of his ideas—and, perhaps, he clutches the table to keep from clutching the throats of the men before him.

A third point concerns what Ayn Rand describes as the "slanted" nature of her writing. She presents the facts of Roark's appearance, his posture, the sound of his voice. But she chooses to leave out countless other facts that can also be observed in that room: the clothes Roark wears, the length of his hair, his rosy complexion from the cold of the streets, the wallpaper, the carpet, the paintings, and a thousand more details. She chooses not to present these details because they do not facilitate the conclusion she wishes the reader to draw. Her focus is selective; she slants or stylizes the writing, presenting only the specific facts the reader needs to draw the right conclusion regarding Roark's emotional state. The reader is provided all the observational evidence he requires, and encumbered with no distracting irrelevancies. He must himself infer the conclusion, just as he would have to were he a board member sitting in that room: Roark is experiencing intense emotion.

A fourth point involves a question. A common objection to Ayn Rand's writing is that it is "unemotional," making it obvious that some readers, like the members of the board, fail to draw the right conclusion. The question is this: Why, given the selective facts with which the readers are presented, do they sometimes see a lack of emotion in Rand's writing? Because Ayn Rand's writing style is as innovative as is Roark's style of design. Most novelists name the emotions their characters experience, providing the reader with the conclusion of the thought process. But Ayn Rand's method necessitates that the reader make the inference himself. A casual reader may miss the point. But one reading Ayn Rand at a maximum effort of mental concentration experiences the intense emotionality of her heroes. The reader, too—in order to fully understand and appreciate *The Fountainhead*—must think independently. Thus, Ayn Rand's writing style is congruent with the novel's theme.

CliffsNotes Review

Use this CliffsNotes Review to test your understanding of the original text, and reinforce what you've learned in this book. After you work through the review and essay questions, identify the quote section, and the fun and useful practice projects, you're well on your way to understanding a comprehensive and meaningful interpretation of *The Fountainhead*.

Q&A

1. The leading example of independence in the novel is:

   a. Ellsworth Toohey

   b. Guy Francon

   c. Ike the Genius

   d. Howard Roark

2. Dominique Francon, in an attempt to end Roark's career, joins forces with:

   a. Austen Heller

   b. Ellsworth Toohey

   c. Henry Cameron

   d. Louise Keating

3. As a means of establishing a collectivist dictatorship in the United States, Toohey goes to work for:

   a. Gail Wynand's newspaper

   b. Guy Francon's architectural firm

   c. Roger Enright's oil company

   d. Catherine Halsey's mission for the poor

4. Which one of the following hires Roark as part of a confidence scheme:

   a. Anthony Cord

   b. Kent Lansing

   c. Caleb Bradley

   d. Austen Heller

5. Dominique's motive in seeking to end Roark's career is:

   a. a form of spiritual murder

   b. a form of spiritual mercy killing

   c. an effort to aid the poor

   d. an attempt to advance her father's career

6. Gail Wynand hires Roark to build his home because:

   a. he wishes to impress the public

   b. he genuinely understands and admires Roark's work

   c. because Roark was Dominique's lover

   d. because Roark needs a job

7. The theme of The Fountainhead is _____.

8. Gail Wynand panders to public taste in his newspapers because _____.

9. Ellsworth Toohey seeks to destroy Roark because _____.

10. Peter Keating gives up Katie for Dominique not because he loves Dominique but because _____.

11. Guy Francon is the most prestigious architect in New York because _____.

12. Despite being the best architect of his time, Henry Cameron is publicly rejected because _____.

Answers: (1) d, (2) b, (3) a, (4) c, (5) b, (6) b, (7) the conflict between independence and dependence, (8) he seeks power over men, (9) there is no room for independent thinkers in the collectivist dictatorship he attempts to establish, (10) Dominique's beauty and elegance impress other people, (11) he gives the public what it is used to and wines and dines prospective clients with impeccable charm and manners, (12) people are afraid of his revolutionary ideas.

Identify the Quote

1. "That was the most selfish thing you've ever seen a man do."

2. "How do you always manage to decide?"

"How can you let others decide for you?"

3. "Always be what people want you to be."

4. "You're not alive. Where's your I?"

"Where's yours?" she asked quietly.

5. "I came here to state that I do not recognize anyone's right to one minute of my life."

Answers: (1) This is Howard Roark speaking to the board of the Manhattan Bank Company. They have accepted his design for a new building contingent on making changes to it. He rejects the commission. (2) This is an exchange between Peter Keating and Howard Roark. Keating asks the first question. Roark responds with a question. (3) This is Keating speaking to Roark at Kiki Holcolmbe's party. (4) This is Keating asking the first question of Dominique. She then replies by asking him the same question. (5) This is Roark speaking to the jury at his trial for the Cortlandt dynamiting.

Essay Questions

1. In what sense is Howard Roark "selfish"? In what sense are Ellsworth Toohey and Peter Keating "selfless"? Discuss the revolutionary nature of Ayn Rand's thinking on this issue.

2. Explain what is meant by the terms "first-hander" and "second-hander." How does the conflict between men of these clashing methods form the novel's theme?

3. Ayn Rand describes her philosophy as one of "man-worship." Explain what she means by this.

4. Conventionally, conformity and nonconformity have been considered opposing methods of conduct. Explain Ayn Rand's reasons for considering them similar.

5. Analyze the character of Dominique Francon. What erroneous premise does she hold, and by what means does she correct it?

6. Explain the way in which Gail Wynand's attempt to combine the contradictory methods of first-handedness and second-handedness leads to his destruction.

7. In asking Roark to design Cortlandt, Keating says he would sell his soul for Roark's help. Roark replies, "To sell your soul is the easiest thing in the world. That's what everybody does every hour of his life. If I asked you to keep your soul—would you understand why that's much harder?" Fully explain the meaning of this scene.

8. Analyze positive minor characters like Steven Mallory, Austen Heller, Mike Donnigan, or those of your choosing and explain how each is a variation on the book's theme. Then do the same with such negative characters as Lois Cook, Gus Webb, and Hopton Stoddard.

Practice Projects

1. Create a Web site to introduce The Fountainhead to other readers. Design pages to intrigue and inform your audience, and invite other readers to post their thoughts and responses to their reading of the novel.

2. Choose a scene from the novel and dramatize it for other classes. The production will require putting the scene in play form, assigning roles, and directing and staging the production. Follow the performance with a discussion of the novel's themes.

3. Debate in class the need to think independently versus the need to be liked by other people. One student or group presents Roark's thinking on this issue, and another student or group presents Keating's.

4. Write a brief letter to the editor of a newspaper or magazine defending Roark's right to his own intellectual property.

5. Discuss in class what human society would be like if Roark's convictions were dominant, if Toohey's were, if Keating's were, if Dominique's were. Have any countries ever been established on the principles held by any of these characters? If so, which ones?

CliffsNotes Resource Center

The learning doesn't need to stop here. CliffsNotes Resource Center shows you the best of the best—links to the best information in print and online about Ayn Rand and related works. And don't think that this is all we've prepared for you; we've put all kinds of pertinent information at www.cliffsnotes.com. Look for all the terrific resources at your favorite bookstore or local library and on the Internet. When you're online, make your first stop www.cliffsnotes.com where you'll find more incredibly useful information about *The Fountainhead.*

Books

This CliffsNotes book provides a meaningful interpretation of *The Fountainhead* published by Hungry Minds, Inc. If you are looking for information about Ayn Rand or related works, check out these other publications.

Critical Works about Rand

Letters of Ayn Rand, edited by Michael Berliner, provides a collection of Ayn Rand's letters, on topics ranging from her philosophy of Objectivism to advice for beginning writers. Also includes an introduction by Leonard Peikoff. New York: Plume, 1997.

The Ayn Rand Lexicon: Objectivism from A to Z, edited by Harry Binswanger, offers an alphabetically arranged collection of Rand's writings on her philosophy of Objectivism. New York: New American Library Trade, 1990.

The Journals of Ayn Rand, edited by David Harriman, provides a personal look at Ayn Rand in her own words. Includes Rand's notes for her writing, essays, and thoughts on Hollywood and communism among other topics. New York: Plume, 1997.

The Ayn Rand Reader, edited by Gary Hull, contains excerpts from all of Rand's novels. Introduces readers to Rand's writing and philosophy. New York: Plume, 1999.

Objectivism: The Philosophy of Ayn Rand, by Leonard Peikoff, offers an explanation of Ayn Rand's philosophy from the renowned Rand scholar. An excellent resource on Rand and her philosophy. New York: Meridian Books, 1993.

The Ominous Parallels, by Leonard Peikoff, explores the causes of Nazism and the parallels between the thought and beliefs in Nazi Germany and the United States. New York: Plume, 1997.

Rand's Major Works of Fiction

Anthem. 1961. New York: Plume, 1999.

Atlas Shrugged. 1957. New York: Signet, 1996.

The Fountainhead. 1943. New York: Signet, 1996.

We the Living. 1936. New York: New American Library, 1996.

The Early Ayn Rand: A Selection from Her Unpublished Fiction. New York: New American Library, 1986.

Rand's Major Works of Nonfiction

Capitalism: The Unknown Ideal. 1967. New York: New American Library, 1984.

For the New Intellectual. 1961. New York: New American Library, 1984.

Introduction to Objectivist Epistemology. Ed. Harry Binswanger and Leonard Peikoff. New York: Meridian Books, 1990.

Philosophy: Who Needs I. 1982. New York: New American Library, 1985.

Return of the Primitive: The Anti-Industrial Revolution. Ed. Peter Schwartz. New York: Meridian Books, 1999.

The Romantic Manifesto. 1971. New York: New American Library, 1975.

Russian Writings on Hollywood. Ed. Michael Berliner. Marina del Ray, California: The Ayn Rand Institute Press, 1999.

The Virtue of Selfishness: A New Concept of Egoism. 1964. New York: New American Library, 1989.

The Voice of Reason: Essays in Objectivist Thought. New York: Meridian Books, 1990.

It's easy to find books published by Hungry Minds, Inc. You'll find them in your favorite bookstores (on the Internet and at a store near you). We also have three Web sites that you can use to read about all the books we publish:

- `www.cliffsnotes.com`
- `www.dummies.com`
- `www.hungryminds.com`

Internet

Check out these Web resources for more information Ayn Rand or *The Fountainhead*:

The Ayn Rand Institute, `aynrand.org` — The Ayn Rand Institute Web site is an outstanding source of information regarding Rand's life, her books, her philosophy of Objectivism, and applications of Objectivism to current events and issues.

Second Renaissance Boos, `www.rationalminds.com` @ md This internet and catalogue marketer features the most complete selection of Ayn Rand's writings and recorded lectures available anywhere. For a free print catalogue, call 1-888-729-6149

Journals of Ayn Rand, `www.capitalism.org/journals/index. html` — The unofficial Web site for the *Journals of Ayn Rand* offers excerpts from the book as well as comments from scholars and readers.

Next time you're on the Internet, don't forget to drop by `www.cliffsnotes.com`. We created an online Resource Center that you can use today, tomorrow, and beyond.

Films and Audio Recordings

Check out these films and audio recordings for more information on Ayn Rand or *The Fountainhead*:

Ayn Rand: A Sense of Life. Dir. Michael Paxton. Perf. Sharon Gless (narrator), Janne Peters, and Peter Sands. AG Media Corporation, Ltd. and Copasetic, Inc., 1997. A documentary film based on Ayn Rand's life.

The Fountainhead. Dir. King Vidor. Perf. Gary Cooper, Patricia Neal, Raymond Massey, and Kent Smith. First National Pictures, Inc. and Warner Brothers, 1949. A feature film based on the novel.

Love Letters. Dir. William Dieterle. Perf. Jennifer Jones and Joseph Cotton. Paramount Pictures, 1945. A feature film written by Ayn Rand.

Rand, Ayn. *The Fountainhead*. 1943. Read by Christopher Hurt. Audiocassette (unabridged). Blackstone Audio Books, 1995.

You Came Along. Dir. John Farrow. Perf. Robert Cummings and Lizabeth Scott. Paramount Pictures, 1945. A feature film written by Ayn Rand.

The preceding films and recordings can be found for sale at Internet bookstores or video stores, or for rent at most local libraries and video stores.

Send Us Your Favorite Tips

In your quest for learning, have you ever experienced that sublime moment when you figure out a trick that saves time or trouble? Perhaps you realized you were taking ten steps to accomplish something that could have taken two. Or you found a little-known workaround that gets great results. If you've discovered a useful tip that helped you study more effectively and you'd like to share it, the CliffsNotes staff would love to hear from you. Go to our Web site at www.cliffsnotes.com and click the Talk to Us button. If we select your tip, we may publish it as part of CliffsNotes Daily, our exciting, free e-mail newsletter. To find out more or to subscribe to a newsletter, go to www.cliffsnotes.com on the Web.

Index

NOTES

NOTES

NOTES

CliffsNotes

LITERATURE NOTES

Check Out the All-New CliffsNotes Guides

TECHNOLOGY TOPICS

PERSONAL FINANCE TOPICS

CAREER TOPICS